FUN WITH IRISH MYTHS

A MUST FOR EVERY IRISHMAN
OR THOSE WHO HAVE TO
LIVE WITH ONE

By John J. Ollivier

TOP OF THE MOUNTAIN PUBLISHING
Largo, Florida 34643-5117 U.S.A.

Fun With Irish Myths
Copyright 1991, John J. Ollivier

Top Of The Mountain Publishing
11701 South Belcher Road, Suite 123
Largo, Florida 34643-5117 USA
SAN 287-590X
FAX 1(813) 536-3681
PHONE 1(813) 530-0110

Library of Congress Cataloging-in-Publication Data
Ollivier, John J.
    Fun with Irish myths / by John J. Ollivier.
    p.   cm.
    "A must for every Irishman or those who have to
live with one."
    ISBN 1-56087-014-1 (quality pbk.) : $11.95
    1. Mythology, Celtic. 2. Ireland—Religion. 3.
National characteristics, Irish. I.Title.
BL980.I7045   1991
398.2'09415—dc20   91-11422 CIP

Manufactured in the United States

Table of Contents

Poetry is indented.
Art is taken from Celtic drawings.

About The Author

John J. Ollivier brings to his books a unique writing style of prose blended with poetry, a wide variety of experiences from a background of teaching, counseling, and building.

John is a light-hearted, sometimes impertinent Irishman and Frenchman mixed into one delightful, quick-minded, humorous individual. His other works include *Fun with Greek Myths, Fun with Nursery Rhymes,* and just completed *Fun with Nordic Myths* and is currently writing *Fun With African Myths.*

He has retired as a teacher/counselor and has now devoted full time to research and writing. Now living in Port Clinton, Ohio, he brings fun back into learning about one's heritage.

John Ollivier's other books may be ordered from
Top Of The Mountain Publishing
11701 S. Belcher Road, #123
Largo, Florida 34643-5117 U.S.A.

Fun With Greek Myths, Hardcover...........$22.95
Fun With Nursery Rhymes, Paperback......$6.95
Please add $2.50 per item for shipping
Write for FREE catalog

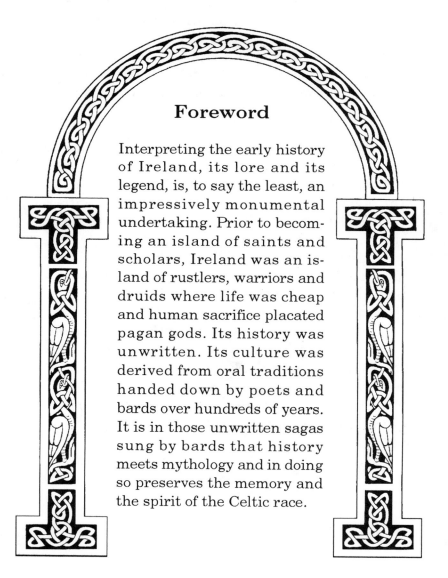

Foreword

Interpreting the early history of Ireland, its lore and its legend, is, to say the least, an impressively monumental undertaking. Prior to becoming an island of saints and scholars, Ireland was an island of rustlers, warriors and druids where life was cheap and human sacrifice placated pagan gods. Its history was unwritten. Its culture was derived from oral traditions handed down by poets and bards over hundreds of years. It is in those unwritten sagas sung by bards that history meets mythology and in doing so preserves the memory and the spirit of the Celtic race.

This book is not an exhaustive treatment of Irish history. It rather deals with Ireland's pre-history where Celtic gods and Irish heroes walked hand in hand in the realm of mythological fancy. It is a compendium of Celtic myths selected by their importance and dealt with fully enough to clarify that importance in Celtic tradition.

The purest enjoyment of this text, however, is contributed by the author, an eloquent story teller himself, in lending his own poetic interpretations to the legendary accounts, punctuating each with a good deal of humor. With a unique understanding of the Irish, he has taken a given set of mythological circumstances and applied to them his own imaginative insights. He then sets each of them to rhyme to amuse, inform and thoroughly entertain the reader.

I believe you will share my enthusiasm for the author's unique and witty poems by which he teaches so effectively. Everyone is proud of one's heritage, perhaps no one more so than the Irish. That's why this book is a must for every Irishman — or those who have to live with one.

Ladonna Cunningham

Introduction

It is difficult to define the mythological world of ancient Celts. At best, one can only attempt to describe it. Even to describe it, one must free oneself from all concepts of classical mythology, for Celtic gods were unlike the gods of the Greeks or Romans. There was no Mount Olympus where Celtic gods presided. They had no home in heaven. There was no Hades. There was not even a hierarchy among Irish deities. Unlike the gods of classical mythology, Celtic gods were not patrons of love or war or art; nor did they have special functions to perform as did the Greek and Roman gods.

Fun with Irish Myths

If Greek mythology developed more perfectly than Celtic mythology it was because of the great poets and sculptors with which the Greeks were blessed. It was their genius that immortalized Greek gods in literature and stone. The Celts were not similarly blessed. Their gods were local in origin. Their names differed in each and every locality where they were worshipped. A single god might have multiple names and often did, especially in the diverse lands occupied by the Celtic people. These ancient Celts dwelled in Britain, Wales, Scotland, Cornwall, and the Isle of Man, as well as in Ireland.

The Irish Celts did acknowledge the "other world," but it was not given much prominence, for gods and men dwelled together on Irish soil in a kind of uneasy partnership. The Greeks thought of their myths historically. The Irish thought of their history mythologically. The paganism of the Irish differed greatly from the paganism of other Indo-Europeans. These ancient gods of Ireland were but pre-historic tribes that once labored and fought on Irish soil and still dwell there, invisibly, side by side with the human inhabitants of that land.

The natural and the supernatural walked hand in hand in Celtic mythology. They deeply penetrated each other in the oral traditions of the ancient Irish. Fortunately, these oral traditions survived long enough to be written down by Christian monks many centuries later.

There was a mythological period in Irish prehistory when events happened that we no longer see, when unsheathed swords related the brave deeds that warriors had done and the Stone of Fal, brought to Ireland by ancient gods, cried out to proclaim the country's lawful king, and Irish wee-people enticed unsuspecting mortals into their underground kingdom of the sid.

It is common to all folklore that the supernatural is natural and the marvelous is normal. Each set of folklore has its own "Once upon a time," when animals spoke and gods became swans or boars or serpents, and spears and arrows always found their mark with an almost divine deftness.

There was a certain dialectic in the Celtic mentality that combined religion and magic. The Irish regarded their gods as master magicians. For them the sacred and the magic were not distinct notions. A certain tension between reality and fantasy characterizes all Celtic literature. At times it is not easy to tell the world of the divine from the world of the human, or the real world of Irish history from the mythological world of the Irish sid.

Myth penetrates reality at almost every turn in Irish tales. It was typical of the Celtic mind to put the cart before the horse. They placed night before day, death before life, evil gods before good gods, the Fir Bolg in Ireland before the Goidels.

Celtic people were free spirits. They had little tolerance for centralized authority, even their own.

Fun with Irish Myths

Ireland, isolated by its geographic location, remained free of Roman colonization, but on the continent the independent and freewheeling Celts were no match for Roman organization. When Caesar defeated the Celtic leader, Versingetorix, at Alesia in 52 B.C., Celtic culture soon disappeared from continental Europe.

It was only in Ireland, never colonized by the Romans, that the Celtic language and culture were carefully preserved. Ireland remained totally untouched by Roman arms and was largely unaffected by Roman civilization. Celtic society did not change appreciably in Ireland until the advent of Christianity and the arrival of the Viking invaders in the fifth century after Christ. The culture and language of the Iron Age Celts survived in Ireland long after it had died out elsewhere.

Thus a study of these ancient Irish tales and myths is necessary to understand the Celtic culture of any age. The aim of this work is to acquaint ourselves with those primitive tales and ancient myths in an effort to understand the Celts of the past and the Irish of today. May our efforts add to your knowledge and contribute to your pleasure and enjoyment.

Celtic Origins

A little bit of heaven's love
    Once fell into the sea.
The island home of Irishmen,
    It soon would come to be.

Someone did chance upon this land,
    To make discovery.
And this they did quite long ago,
    Perhaps by God's decree.

How did they come upon this isle?
    Where did they find its key?
The story of brave journeys there,
    Is Celtic history.

Four hundred years before Our Lord,
    The Celts had reached their peak.
Their influence in Europe, though,
    Never equaled that of Greek.

Celts made their mark most patently,
    In England, Gaul and Spain.
But German tribes that roamed the north
    Their power did constrain.

Where did these Celts first journey from?
    Bohemia, they say!
They took a lot of side trips, though,
    'Fore reaching Gallway Bay.

A Unique Problem
with Celtic Myths

Ireland was first mentioned in the Geography of Ptolemy nearly three hundred years before Our Lord. About 500 B.C. Hecataeus referred to the people of central Europe as Celts. Greeks called them Hyperboreans. The name "Keltoi" was first used by the Greeks as "Gaulish" was first used by the Romans to depict Celtic people in literature. But archaeological discoveries treat the Celts much earlier than literature does.

Celts inhabited Europe in pre-Roman times from Ireland to Romania. Archaeological studies reveal that Celts appeared at the beginning of the Iron Age, about 1000 B.C. They soon became the most dominant people of non-Mediterranean Europe. Their culture rapidly became the flower of the Iron Age. Although these barbarians shook the foundations of all the states of antiquity, they themselves formed no state of lasting importance.

Their homeland was probably Bohemia, from which they moved westward into northern Italy, Gaul, Spain, Britain, and Ireland. They moved eastward into Turkey and threatened the empire of Alexander the Great. By 390 B.C. they had sacked Rome. Ninety-three years later they desecrated the temple at Delphi. Those Celts that remained in Asia Minor were known as Galatians. It was to them that

St. Paul addressed his Epistle. Many of them later marched west and settled in France where Romans called them Gauls.

Celtic culture reached its peak about 500 B.C., a hundred years before history first mentioned any of the Germanic tribes. This Celtic culture was the very foundation of Europe's past. It was the root of western history. The fact that Celts had no written language presents a unique problem in the study of their mythology.

Druids forbade a written language in order to keep their cultic mysteries hidden, or more probably, to guarantee their own druidic future. By such restrictions they made certain that their cast was needed and their importance continued. With no written language all past traditions, teachings, and culture were memorized by druids and handed down orally by poets. Thus druids and poets were treasured by this Celtic society that regarded its laws, its genealogies, and its history as sacred as its religion.

With no written language, there was no written history. For this reason, much of the Celtic past is a mystery that escapes us. Early knowledge of Celtic mythology is only fragmentary as gleaned from monuments and inscriptions and the various classical authors who spoke of them. In Gaul, Celtic mythology was lost beyond any recovery, since there the Celtic language was wiped out by Roman conquest and a history was all but forgotten. But where their Celtic language lived on as in Ireland is where those oral teachings and traditions were preserved and handed down by bard and poet until received and written down many centuries later by Irish monks.

A flamboyant aristocracy, developed among the Celts in Ireland, was extolled in their ballads and poems for countless centuries. It was this folk memory that the Irish monks transcribed in writing some eight centuries after Christ to preserve it for posterity. These ancient Irish myths are now listed among the world's oldest recorded stories.

It was not surprising, however, that these same Irish monks sought to baptize Ireland's pagan past by deleting from it that which was offensive to the faith and by adding to it that which might be more beneficial. We must face the obvious fact that we received these myths from men with conflicting loyalties, whose spiritual aim was to eliminate the very religious system which gave birth to that mythology. A glossary of a twelfth-century scribe clearly suggests such a prejudice.

"But I who have written this history, or rather fable, am doubtful about many things, for some of them are the figments of demons, some of them poetic imaginings, some true, some not, some for delight of fools."

One must always begin at the beginning. Thus every mythology should involve a cosmology. This, however, was not the case with Irish mythology. We find no Celtic creation myths tracing Irish origins back to primitive gods. There is a conspicuous absence of any Irish cosmology. Perhaps it was conveniently forgotten by Irish monks as offensive to pious ears, or perhaps it was doctored in some way to bring Ireland's pagan past into conformity with the biblical account of creation and make the Irish people descendants of Adam before the flood and of Noah following it.

If there were a doctoring of Celtic mythology by Irish monks and scribes, it was completed by the twelfth century in the "Lebor Gabala Eirann," The Book of Conquests of Ireland, in which the arrival of the Gaels was the last of a series of invasions. Whatever the case, any study of Irish mythology must proceed from the ambiguous to the unknown. The study of Celtic mythology leaves us with more questions than answers. Any search for the beginnings of Irish civilization will always be surrounded by serious doubts. And yet in spite of the problems that surround it, the search must be undertaken. We must make an earnest effort to overcome these difficulties and penetrate the elusive mystery of those ancient Celts who first peopled Ireland, for from that little island those same Celts have peopled the world with their numerous and marvelous descendants.

Celtic Myths

These Celtic myths and fairy tales
    Are in themselves unique.
They differ much from other myths,
    A difference we seek.

There is no Mount Olympus
    Where Irish gods abide,
Nor Nordic Hall Valhalla,
    For heroes that have died.

There is no hierarchy,
    Where Zeus stands at the fore.
The Celtic myths are different
    From all that went before.

These Celtic gods were tribal gods,
    Not everywhere adored.
They had no home in heaven's court,
    From which they were implored.

Abnormal were these ancient gods,
    Some dwarfs with heads of goats,
Some giants with one hand and foot,
    Which fear in all promotes.

They called their gods Formorians,
    Great gods of death and storm,
The opposite of Grecian gods,
    In genesis and form.

Thus darkness came ere Celtic light,
  Night came before the day.
And evil came before the good.
  It was the Irish way.

This is unique to Irish myths,
  And to the Irish mind.
The cart is placed before the horse.
  The horse is placed behind.

The Greeks made myths their history.
  The Celts made history myths.
Their ancient gods were ancient Celts,
  Who fought with spears and fists.

Their gods were pre-historic tribes,
  Who dwelled there long ago.
And still live there invisibly,
  On earth, and just below.

All Irish are a mystery,
  Their wit and smiling eyes.
They trace a Celtic history,
  And history never lies.

When did the Irish first appear?
  How did they find their Isle?
And what's the source of Irish wit?
  And of the Irish smile?

Fun with Irish Myths

No one had heard of Irishmen.
　　None lived upon this land.
A thousand years before Saint Pat
　　No Irish were on hand.

They must have crossed the deep blue sea
　　To come to Ireland.
But it's a lie that they were met
　　By MacNamara's Band.

Everyone's part Irish now,
　　At least they claim to be.
There usually is a Pat or Mike
　　In every family tree.

And every kid with reddish hair
　　Or freckles on his face,
Is said to be descended from
　　The ancient Irish race.

But what about the blue-eyed blonds
　　Found on the Emerald Isle?
I guess Leif Ericsson stopped by
　　For just a little while?

All this shall be the subject of
　　The book you hold in hand.
I think, though, only Irishmen,
　　Will fully understand.

The Celt

Before we enter into a more detailed study of Celtic gods, we must examine more thoroughly the Celtic life and the Celtic personality. A study of each will tell us something about the Celtic mind. And knowledge of the Celtic mind will tell us much about the gods they worshipped, for either the Celtic mind was such because of Celtic gods or Celtic gods were such because of the Celtic mind.

The Celts were Indo-Europeans. They were ancestors of the present day Irish, Scots, Gauls, Welsh, Cornish, Bretons, and Manx. They surfaced in Europe about 1000 B.C. They had no written language, no history, no dominant cities and yet no barbarian people had greater influence on future history, nor was any barbarian people more fully discussed by those who replaced them. The Greeks referred to those who spoke no civilized language as barbarian. Ephorus listed four such nations some four hundred years before Christ: Libyans in Africa, Persians to the East, Scythians to the north, and the Celts in Europe.

The Celts were a very superstitious people. They conceived of spirits everywhere, in trees, in rocks, in rivers and bogs. Through the study of archaeology and the reports of classical authors over four hundred Celtic gods are known. Of those names, three hundred occur only once. The supernatural pervaded every phase of Celtic life. Their gods were shadowy figures, not in any way clearly ordered like the gods of Greeks or Romans. Yet these gods controlled the seasons of the year and every aspect of nature. If Celts were troubled with danger or disease, it was due to gods who were wrathful in revenge. Often times these gods had to be placated through intermediaries like druids who knew ancient wisdom and procedures. In order to save a life, another life had to be surrendered. Criminals and captives of war were preferred victims, but when they were wanting, innocent men and even children were substituted. Fathers had the right of life or death over their children in Celtic society. Each tribe had its own tribal god and each tribal god had his own goddess consort.

Celts were fluid in their tribal life. It was not uncommon for whole tribes to move across vast territories. They had an innate love of wandering. They were basically a restless people. And because of their vivid and original imaginations, they were born rebels against any existing order. They wanted and demanded war to make things perfect. Although they moved about frequently, they had a common cultural affinity and common language. They shared a common calendar and a mode of life highly influenced by druids. Cows were most important to these ancient Celts and served as a means of exchange. Since they were so valuable in Celtic life, raids were common and stealing cows was a valuable means of increasing one's wealth or power. Circumstances surrounding these raids often served as the foundation for Irish tales and myths.

The tribe was the center of Celtic life. It was all important. Although marriages were always outside the individual family, they were never outside the tribe, except in the case of the king. When children were born into the Celtic family, their education was placed in the care of someone outside the family, but not outside the tribe. "Fostering," the practice of placing children in the care of another for their upbringing, became the principle of Celtic life and education. A boy would not return home until he was seventeen. A girl returned home at the age of fourteen. Ties between foster brothers and foster fathers were very close and binding and played a very important part in Celtic life even after the child returned home.

We must view the ancient Celt living in an established society which he himself had helped form, and yet he himself was formed in many ways by that same society. The typical Celt had a quick and agile mind with a love of riddles. He had an almost excessive penchant for brightly colored clothing. His favorite pastime was love, intoxication, music, poetry, chariot races, but especially war. Herodotus described the Celt as "tall with light skin and hair and eyes, boastful and vainglorious, but demonic in battle, fond of hunting and feasting, and music and poetry, and glittering jewelry and bright colors."

They were known as exceptional storytellers but very prone to exaggeration. Plato referred to them as "drunken and combative."

Classical observers considered Celts quite susceptible to magic and melancholy. They were judged to be eloquent and of lyric genius. They were volatile in temperament, easily given to reckless extravagance, and contentiousness. Personal looks were of great concern to them. To be fat was socially unacceptable. Celtic women used mirror and tweezers to pluck their hair. Women used makeup to appear more beautiful and men painted their bodies to appear more frightening. A man's hair was swept back; his mustache drooped.

It was this pagan Celt that in some way modified the gods that he worshipped and in turn was modified by them. Religion and life always walk hand in hand and greatly influence each other. This was certainly the case with Celtic life and the Celtic religion. Celts had no temples. They worshipped their gods in woodlands. They lived in the midst of the supernatural and defended themselves against that supernatural by force or by magic. The human and the divine constantly intermingled and shared the land. There was no beyond. There was no elsewhere.

The Ancient Celts

The Celts were called "barbarian."
    They didn't speak in Greek.
But what did old Ephorus know?
    Why judge by his critique?

Who were these Celts? Whence did they come?
    What made them change address?
Who led them to their island home?
    Were they rich or penniless?

The Celt was a religious man,
    Barbarian at heart.
So human sacrifice in cult
    Played an important part.

Those Celts were superstitious, though,
    In worshipping their god.
And their druidic clergymen,
    As heathens were quite odd.

Why were their gods so numerous?
    Why'd each god have a wife?
And were those gods so barbarous
    That they'd demand a life?

Teutates were their gods of tribe,
    Adored by different names.
And mortals killed in sacrifice
    Their anger overcame.

Fun with Irish Myths

What good was human sacrifice?
　　What blessings could it bring
To deity or victims of
　　This human butchering?

These savage rites do indicate
　　A worship in excess.
At least they seem to indicate
　　A godly wantonness.

And why were cows so valuable,
　　That rustling was condoned?
And why were children boarded out
　　Until they were full-grown?

And what about the way of life
　　That Celts were won't to live?
Why were carousings and their wars,
　　A Celt prerogative?

Their storytelling and their songs,
　　Were special Celtic traits,
Embellished with each telling,
　　As history indicates.

These are the questions we must ask,
　　If knowledge is to grow.
And we must answer each of them
　　To leave the "status quo."

Some will ignore these questions asked,
    And bigotry display.
They will condemn all Irishmen,
    Cause some are made of clay.

I'm sure that some will quickly sneer,
    When reading of the past,
"I know of present Irishmen,
    Who's life is still a blast."

"They fight and drink like lushes.
    They're given to the booze.
They misuse every gift they have,
    And then they sing the blues."

But those who say such silly things,
    Are envious, I'm sure.
They wish that they were Irishmen,
    Instead of immature.

You'll find the average Irishman,
    Is really very nice.
But if you dare insult a Celt,
    You'll have to pay the price.

We always see another's faults,
    Unless we are quite blind.
I'm sure the Irish have a few,
    They're just too hard to find.

The Celtic Warrior

As enemies the Greeks feared the Celts, but as neighbors they were quite curious about them and observed them rather closely. One such observation was expressed by Strabo who stated that the whole race of Celts, which he called Gallic or Galatic, "is madly fond of war, high spirited, quick to battle, but otherwise straightforward and not of evil character. And so when they are stirred up they assemble in their bands for battle, quite openly and without forethought so that they are easily handled by those who desire to outwit them; for at any time or place and on whatever pretext you stir them up, you will have them ready to face danger, even if they have nothing on their side but their own strength."

Aristotle used the example of Celts to discuss the nature of bravery. Above all else the Celt was a warrior. And so we must study this aspect of Celtic life to understand the Celts. Celtic warriors were hot-headed and excitable. "The whole race is war-mad." The easily provoked Celt, however, proved no match in battle for the cold Romans, although as we know from classical writers, the Romans were much impressed by the effectiveness of the chariot in Celtic warfare.

Chariots were in use in many cultures, but the Celts made the chariot a war machine. The chariot driven by a wild- haired Celt was a favorite motif for coins. "The chariots were two wheeled, strong in structure, and quite lethal in trained hands."

The weapons of the Celtic warrior were a long sword, a long shield, a spear, which was a kind of javelin, and a wooden weapon like a "grossphus" which was thrown by hand. They had bows and slings but they were not very important and were seldom used. An oval shield made of wicker work or planks covered most of the warrior's naked body. He held it in his left hand, leaving his right hand free for fighting the enemy.

Helmets were topped with projecting figures to make the wearer look larger. "They wore helmets like the head and gaping jaws of terrible wild beasts and other strange creatures in an effort to frighten their opponents." The Irish were extremely superstitious. Neck torques were worn by all warriors and had the magical significance that the torque would protect the fighting Celt from harm.

Noise was an important part of the Celtic warfare technique. Warriors yelled and screamed and beat their carts and wagons and blew their trumpets to frighten a confused enemy. Their trumpets were of a peculiar barbaric kind which when blown into would produce a very harsh sound which added greatly to the tumult of war.

Intra-tribal differences were often settled by warfare. The bravest challenge was to single combat with one's opponent. When the challenge was accepted, each warrior recited the valor of his ancestors and his own past glories in battle and then downgraded the skills of his opponent.

Free men served as charioteers and shield bearers for nobles in battle. The horse was essential in war as well as in peace. The Irishmen's special love and appreciation of the horse can be seen in Celtic graves and on Celtic coins. The horse was widely used on farms in time of peace by many different people about 700 B.C., but the Celts were the first to make the horse play such an important part in time of war. Celtic swords and lances were fashioned for fighting from a horse. The Celtic notion of charioteering soon overshadowed the common idea of fighting from horseback. Charioteering was truly a Celtic institution, and the Celtic warrior was thoroughly skilled in its method of warfare.

The Fighting Irish

I'm sure if you know Irishmen
    You know they love to fight.
Don't think an Irish altar boy
    Is just an acolyte.

He's probably on the schoolyard grounds,
    At war with other boys.
And if he's true unto his past,
    He's making lots of noise.

He often takes on far more odds,
    Than prudence says he should,
But like ancestral counterparts
    This is misunderstood.

The Irish battle many fights,
    With brawn instead of brains.
Their bravery beclouds their thought,
    As danger it disdains.

I think we are quire fortunate,
    Chariots went out of style.
Or else we'd see those Irish kids
    Astride them with a smile.

All charging loudly down the street,
    With red hair wildly flung,
And with a torque around their neck,
    As mothers come unstrung.

31

Fun with Irish Myths

For horses Celts became unglued,
    Almost like maniacs.
And their descendants still today,
    Are found at all the tracks.

We see their flare for colors bright,
    In clothes that jockeys wear.
They've mellowed since their warrior days,
    Or they'd be riding bare.

The Celts of old were drinking men,
    Who killed with just one blow.
They wanted heads upon their ale,
    But not upon their foe.

I'm sure that each of us can see
    In every modern Celt,
Some semblance of their bygone days
    That nature's clearly dealt.

Quick tempers fly, quick wits excel,
    Exaggerations flourish,
A special love of pork and spuds,
    Their favorite things that nourish.

Yes, Irishmen reflect their past,
    Ancestry's yesteryears,
Flamboyancy, yet tenderness,
    That often shows in tears.

The Irish King

Ancient Irish society was aristocratic. There were no cities. Cruacha and Emmain Macha were not cities, but compounds where the king lived. It was here he entertained his many chieftains with feasts, poets, singers, musicians, jugglers and annual assemblies at which games were held.

The Irish "Tuatha" or tribe was ruled by a king through a general assembly of people which met once a year in a field among ancestral tombs. Celtic society was divided into three classes. The class of nobles consisted of warriors, bards, druids, jurists, men of learning, and craftsmen. The class of free commoners was composed of farmers and lesser craftsmen. The class of the unfreed consisted of slaves, laborers, the subjugated and those who had been degraded. A king presided over all.

Kingship was sacred to the Celts. Kings in their mythological tales are barely more than euhemerized gods. The tribal king was quite often depicted as married to a tribal goddess. The quality of the king determined the fertility of the land. If a king were healthy and virile and without blemish, the land was fertile. If he were weak or morally blemished, the land was barren.

It was for this reason that the Irish were so intolerant of imperfection, especially in their leaders. If a king were imperfect, either physically

33

ly, he was forced to abdicate. Nuada, though an exceptionally capable king, was forced to abdicate when he lost an arm in battle. Bres, who replaced him, although physically without blemish, soon demonstrated moral imperfection in that he lacked an attribute so characteristic of and so demanded by the Irish. He lacked a spirit of generosity and hospitality. "No matter how often his chiefs visited him their breaths did not smell of ale." Kings were expected to distribute wealth to their chieftains in return for their military service and loyalty. It was for this reason that they had to constantly accumulate more wealth by expansion.

The king was elected from the descendants of a great-grandfather. Thus four generations were eligible for election. Although the king was the trustee, all land was held in common by the local tribe. All shared in inheritances and all shared in fines that might be levied against a tribe by a conquering enemy.

Irish Society

An inhospitable Irishman,
   Simply cannot be.
The very meaning of the words
   Is contradictory.

The Irish might have other faults,
   And I am sure they do.
But service is their heritage.
   I know this to be true.

We find this in their tribal kings,
   Their rulers of the past.
Around this ancient royalty,
   The tribal heart was cast.

The king was treated like a god,
   By druid caste or slave
The warriors and the chieftains too,
   To king their service gave.

But all demanded much of kings,
   For subjects' loyalty.
Perfection was required of him,
   To be "His Royalty."

For if they had a virile king,
   A fertile crop they'd reap.
But if the king were weak or cruel,
   The harvesters would weep.

Fun with Irish Myths

King Bres, himself, was such a king.
    He hated art and letter.
He was a most oppressive king,
    So things would get no better.

He claimed the milk of hairless cows,
    Then issued this decree:
"All Munster cows must pass through fire."
    Which made them all hair free.

If the king were not hospitable,
    To chieftains by his side,
Or didn't give them ale to drink,
    There'd soon be regicide.

All leaders then should learn from this,
    How others should be treated.
Unless they learn it very well,
    They soon will be defeated.

To rule, we know, is but to serve.
    To serve is but to rule.
To learn this fundamental truth,
    We need not go to school.

We learn it through experience,
    The very best of teachers.
And unless we learn it well,
    It could be our impeacher.

The Celtic Feast

Central to Celtic life was the Celtic feast. It built community as it brought kings and people and chieftains together. At these feasts the Celts relived past glories and enjoyed the largess of their leaders. Kings were expected to distribute wealth to their chieftains as well as entertain them.

The cauldron was the focal point of the feast, pointing out symbolically that kings must provide for their people. Drink was all important to the feast. The drink of the wealthy was wine imported from Italy. The drink of the lower class was beer made from wheat and honey. Zythos mentioned that the Celts "were exceedingly fond of wine. When deprived of it they concocted a drink of barley." Polybus was impressed with the Celtic capacity for alcohol:

"They drink a little at a time, not more than a mouthful, but they do it rather frequently."

Drink from the common cup emphasized community. A slave carried the cup from one to the other. Every house had its hearth, its cauldron, and its spit. A variety of foods was served at every feast, especially fish and salted pork. Pork was the Irishman's first love, even in death, as a whole pig was buried with him.

At the Celtic feast sponsored by the king or a chieftain, brave warriors reminisced the past and planned the future. Heroes and kings were praised by professional bards who recited from memory past traditions and sagas. Bards and lyric poets often sang accompanied by the lyre. Chieftains always had in their company companions called parasites who announced the praises of their lords.

The Celtic feast was an institution vital to the ordered function of the community. The feast was filled with noisy, drunken, bombastic, exaggerated boasting and dangerous threats. The bravest warrior merited the finest cut of meat. If someone else claimed it, they fought unto death. Life was cheap at banquet boastings. Seating arrangement was most important and even critical.

Single combat at feasts was common. The cut of meat testified to the valor and worth or status of the warrior and so it could always be challenged by another warrior. These boastings and challenges were a common theme in Celtic tales and Irish myths as we shall see in the story of Mac Da Tho's pig.

Celtic Feasting

The ancient Irish liked to brag,
    About past things they did,
About the glories of their feasts,
    And pigs cooked on the grid.

At all their feasts they loved to drink,
    And get intoxicated,
And fight about who'd cut the meat,
    And pieces allocated.

They were concerned where each should sit.
    This echoed many things.
It pointed to the bravest Celt,
    And favorite of the king.

Most every house had hearth and spit,
    And cauldron that was full.
And where at table each did sit,
    Determined who had pull.

The Irish truly loved their pork.
    It was their favorite food.
And if you've met some Irishmen,
    This same you will conclude.

They seemed a bit impressed with praise,
    And wanted much of it.
Kings hired bards to laud their deeds,
    Their glories to transmit.

Fun with Irish Myths

We get the word called "parasite"
    From Irish hangers on.
At times you still can find them,
    The sycophant or fawn.

So when you're with an Irishman,
    Yes, even to this day.
Just check the signs of bygone Celts,
    And see it's still that way.

I think they feel insecure
    And need esteem from others.
They fail to realize their worth,
    Not told by Irish mothers.

Such shyness is an inbred fault,
    Though this they will deny.
But actions soon belie their words.
    And shyness certify.

Irish Storytellers

Storytelling was a favorite pastime of Irish Celts. They came to believe that eloquence was more powerful than physical strength. Celts were illiterate until the fifth century A.D. It was only through the spoken word that thoughts and traditions were transmitted. Celts depicted their society in the stories they told. All Celts had an innate conservatism for past glories. The very tales that they told were a kind of wishful thinking, if not a propaganda, for past glories.

Irish life, depicted in the stories of the Ulster Cycle, was very similar to the life of the Gaulish society as depicted by Caesar. Stories were usually of love, drunkenness, music, chariot races, but especially war. These were subjects of their tales because they were subjects of their everyday life. Stories were often added to and changed when told and retold. Perhaps these stories have been distorted by translations or politics throughout the ages; perhaps they have been altered by Church censorship; but whatever the case, they must have been embellished time and time again as a challenge to the Irish spirit of exaggeration. Whatever the reality, the tales we are about to examine are studied more for the amusement contained within them than for any historic truth without. They are studied more for entertainment than for fact.

The First Irishmen

There was no room on Noah's ark,
    For Noah's son called Bith.
So Bith and daughter Cessair then,
    Developed their own myth.

They built three ships and sailed west,
    Two met adversity.
The third arrived on Irish shores,
    An island in the sea.

Ladhra and Fintan were aboard,
    With fifty pretty maidens.
The men divided up the maids,
    With which this ship was ladened.

Ladhra and Bith took sixteen wives,
    And Fintan took the others.
So family life sure flourished then,
    As kids had lots of mothers.

King Ladhra with his sixteen wives,
    Was first to rule Erin.
He ruled until the deluge came,
    Which made the land quite barren.

His heart was not upon his job,
    As king, he was a lemon.
"The Book of Conquests" briefly states:
    "He died from excess of women."

Others say that Ladhra died,
    This pilot of Bith's ship,
As oar went up his buttocks,
    Clean up unto its grip.

This sure would smart with lots of pain,
    And cause a funny strut.
And drive an Irishman to drink,
    With pole clean up his butt.

He was the very first to die,
    Perhaps the first drunk, too.
but then the deluge flooded all,
    To start all things anew.

All Irish drowned as deluge came,
    Except the man named Fintan.
He was to live for centuries more,
    Till Patrick came from Britain.

He'd transmigrate as bird and fish,
    Through many future ages.
Becoming self when Patrick came,
    To tell past history's pages.

Ancestors to the Irishmen,
    Were these that all died out.
And not again till Partholon,
    Would Irish gadabout.

Partholon

Two hundred and sixty-eight years after the deluge. On the first of May, the feast of Beltene, who was god of the dead and father of Partholon, Partholon landed on the southwest coast of the Emerald Island. He was a distant descendant of Magog, son of Iafeth. He was a Celt who came to Ireland from Scotland with one thousand men and women. They soon numbered four times that. Partholon was the Celtic god of vegetation. He was not a single god, but an entire race of gods. Partholon and his followers were the first inhabitants to clear the land and till the soil and reap a harvest.

Acasbel was the steward of Partholon. It was Acasbel who built the first guest house. At this time there were many firsts in Ireland. Brea built the first dwelling and made the first cauldron. Malaliach brewed the first beer and was the first to introduce sacrifice and ritual. It was at this time that fostering was first introduced as the basis of Irish education. Bachorbladhra was the first foster-father. Biobal was the first to introduce gold to Ireland, Babel the first to introduce cattle. It was in the time of Partholon that adultery was committed for the first time in Ireland. Partholon left his wife alone with his servant Toba. Toba wronged him. Partholon demanded his honor price, but his wife

Elgnat replied it was she who was entitled to compensation, for an owner must protect his property.

The race of Partholon fought the first battle in Ireland. It was a bitter battle against the wicked Formorians. The Formorians were native powers or gods who were constantly at war with civilized races of men. They were gods of evil, gods of darkness and night, gods of ignorance. They were enemies of arts and letters. They were a race of demons descended from Shem. Some of the Formorians were dwarfs. Some were deformed men with goat heads. Some were giants. Others were monsters with one hand and one foot. They were the acknowledged gods of the Fir Bolg, the Fir Damnann, and the Galion. Their domination in Ireland did not end until the Tuatha De Danann invaded and conquered them.

The supernatural in Irish mythology was a wanton power which assumed a very menacing character. This is clearly seen in the savage rites and rituals of Celtic cults. The Formorians had lived on the coastal islands of Ireland for two hundred years before Partholon. They were often defeated by their many enemies, but they never laid down their arms. Like the powers of chaos they remained ever latent in nature and always hostile to the cosmic order.

Celtic gods often appeared to men under the form of birds. The gods of light were birds of lovely plumage and travelled in pairs. The gods of darkness, the Formorians, appeared as crows and ravens. The wife of Tethra was often seen as a female crow flying over battlefields, picking at the headless bodies of the dead.

Partholon fought Cichol, a Formorian giant, in single combat at the battle of Mag Itha. Cichol killed him. Following Partholon's death, his two sons, Fer and Fergnia, fought the country's first duel to determine which son would replace his father as ruler of Ireland.

As the race of Partholon arrived on the feast of Beltene, so also it was on that feast that the entire race of partholon was destroyed through a mysterious plague. All died in this plague except a man named Tuan Mac Cairill. He survived this and many other existences that he might live long enough to tell his story to St. Patrick.

The Days of Partholon

Young Partholon was Beltene's son
    A Celt who came from Scotland,
To Ireland with a thousand men,
    Though history might "forgot" one.

He came in flight from native land,
    Where he had been most errant.
In seeking to be king of Scots
    He coldly killed both parents.

His brief reign witnessed many firsts,
    That future Celts would cheer,
Both sacrifice and ritual cults,
    And Ireland's first beer.

Then fostering was introduced,
    Where others raise your brats,
And teach them very many things
    To be aristocrats.

The battle of Mag Itha saw,
    Brave Partholon then slain.
He fought the giant Cichol and
    His efforts were in vain.

Ambitious sons fought at his death
    Engaging in a duel.
The reason for this fratricide?
    To see which one would rule!

Fun with Irish Myths

The gods they called Formorians
　　Were evil gods and giants.
And living side by side with men
　　They always were defiant.

These gods had but a single arm,
　　And but a single leg.
This made it tough for playing drums
　　Or running from a plague.

Once when these gods pursued revenge,
　　Mankind was in a barrel.
All humans died in just one week,
　　Except Tuan Mac Cairill.

He somehow lived till Patrick came,
　　To tell him all of this.
To tell of Ireland's glorious past,
　　Its ancient genesis.

Non-Irish might not believe this stuff.
　　But that's too bad for them.
Unless one's life has fantasy,
　　It's really very grim.

This is the very reason why
　　The Irish have such fun.
Their fancy's working overtime,
　　So it won't be outdone.

So many of these ancient Celts
    Had much to tell St. Pat.
And lived a long time after death,
    So they might have their chat.

This Partholon, ancestor to
    All born on Erin's shore
Was rated as an Irish god,
    The primogenitor.

I've never met an Irish kid,
    That was called Partholon.
And if some mother gave that name,
    He had a funny one.

For Partholon O'Reilly seems,
    A little bit depressive.
A Mike or Pat or Brigit sounds,
    I'd say, far more impressive.

So if you are an Irishman,
    And one day have a son,
When choosing what to call your boy,
    Don't call him Partholon.

And even though when this king reigned,
    The world was given beer.
Forget this fact and give your kid
    A name he'll love to hear.

Nemed

Nemed was a nephew of Partholon. He was the son of Agnoman, Partholon's brother. Nemed lead an expedition of thirty-four boats from Greece to Ireland. They were at sea for a year and a half before Nemed arrived on Irish shores. Each of the ships contained thirty people. All the ships sank at sea. There were nine survivors who reached Ireland. They soon increased to four thousand and thirty of each men and women.

Nemed fought four battles against the demonic Formorians. He won all four. He slew two of the Formorian kings, Gend and Sengand. Nemed died from the plague shortly thereafter. His followers suffered much at the hands of the evil Formorian gods, especially under their wicked king, Conann, son of Febor, who ruled from Conann's Tower on Tory Island off the coast of Donegal. This was the ancestral home of the Formorians.

At the time of Conann the descendants of Nemed were ruled by three chiefs, Erglann, Semul, and Fergus. Conann's rule was so oppressive that it led to a revolt. Sixty thousand descendants of Nemed led by their three chiefs march against the evil Formorian king and Fergus killed Conann in battle.

Conann's friend Morc, son of Dele, avenged Conann's death. Only thirty of the sixty thousand that had marched against Conann escaped death. From that time on, Nemed's followers became vassals of the Formorians and had to pay a tribute to them. This tax was levied on each first of November, the feast of Samhain, the symbol of death, as summer ends and winter begins. On that day the descendants of Nemed paid in tribute to the Formorians two-thirds of their corn, milk, and children. This was an annual sacrificial offering to the ominous and blood-thirsty Formorians. The children were sacrificed to Cromm Cruach, the Bloody Head, a great idol worshipped by Celts.

The descendants of Nemed finally rose up against the Formorians but were defeated by them. Again only thirty survived and they set sail in two ships to escape from Ireland. One ship sailed to Greece. The other sailed to the northern most part of the world. Fergus and Briton went to England and there became the ancestors of all Britons. Their descendants remained there until the Saxons arrived and drove them to the border islands. Briton gave his name to the land which it still bears today. At that time the pre-Goidelic Irish spoke the same Celtic dialect as the Britons spoke.

The Days of Nemed

Brave Nemed tried again to gain
    What Partholon abandoned.
So leaving Grecian paradise,
    On Irish shores he landed.

Most all his men were lost at sea,
    As every boat did sink.
A few survived and reached the beach.
    The rest went down the drink.

Those nine survivors of the storm
    Soon grew to quite a number.
And working hard to clear the land,
    There wasn't time for slumber.

Four brothers built a massive moat,
    In just a single day.
The next day Nemed slaughtered them,
    Lest him their strength betray.

For with such strength he feared that they
    Might soundly cook his goose.
He could not let such forcefulness,
    Go prowling on the loose.

Destroying others to succeed,
    Is simply viciousness.
Or else it's insecurity,
    For those so little blessed.

If one has talent he'll succeed,
    Without destroying others.
He will excel because he's skilled,
    Not by betraying brothers.

There are two ways to victory
    In anything we do.
By cheating, as the weak of mind,
    Or by a brilliant coup.

Formorians harassed these men,
    So Nemed slew their kings.
King Conann made them suffer much,
    Till Fergus clipped his wings.

Then Morc avenged King Conann's death,
    And slaughtered Nemed's heir,
And laid a tribute on them all,
    Which led them to despair.

Two thirds of corn and milk and kids,
    Was what they had to pay.
At Cromm Cruach their kids were killed
    On every Samhain Day.

Then Nemed's race in anger fought
    Against these vile Formorians,
But lost the battle and the war,
    According to historians.

Fun with Irish Myths

Just thirty of great Nemed's heirs
    Survived this ugly battle.
Some travelled north, some sailed for Greece
    Forsaking corn and cattle.

King Nemed's son named Britan Mael,
    Would later win much fame.
For it was from this noble man
    That Britons took their name.

The progeny of Semeon,
    Worked Grecian earthenware,
But were enslaved by ruling Greeks,
    Which really wasn't fair.

They had to carry stones in bags,
    In total slavery.
Until they turned their bags to ships,
    And sailed in bravery.

If you must face adversity,
    Don't act like Nemed's race.
Don't run from it like cowards do,
    But stand up to its face.

And when you do, you'll conquer it.
    To learn this, you must do.
So try it and discover what,
    You knew not hitherto.

The Laginian Invasion

Two hundred and thirty years after the death of Nemed, five kings came to Ireland accompanied by their subjects. The five kings were brothers, the five sons of Del. These kings were the progeny of Beotach, son of Iarbonel. They were Slaine, Gann, Sengann, Genann, and Rudraige. They divided the land into fifths. This is the origin of the five provinces of Ireland.

The Fir Bolg had one king. He and his men settled in Ulster. The Fir Damnann had three kings. They settled in Munster, Connacht, and Mide. The Galion had one king. His name was Slane. He settled in Leinster. Slane was chosen chief king by his brothers. All had descended from Semeon.

The followers of these kings were later called Lagin, descendants of Labraid. When Labraid's father, Ailill, was killed by Cobthach, he fled to Gaul, gathered an army, and returned to kill Cobthach and thirty other kings. He thus became king of all of Ireland. He married Moriath. This was the people who inhabited Ireland about 325 B.C. They were called Fir Bolg, Erainn, and Inverni.

The Fir Bolg were off-shoots of the Belgae or Continental Celts. They introduced the spear head of iron. It was they who introduced monarchy to Ireland. The word "Fir Bolg" means men of bags. The Fir Bolg had fled from Ireland to Greece where they were mistreated and forced to carry dirt in leather bags up rocky hills. They finally made boats out of the leather and set out again for Ireland.

Bolg was the god Daire. Lugaid was Daire's son. Daire was the ultimate ancestor god of the other-world. The Fir Bolg, the Fir Damnann and the Fir Galion occupied Ireland jointly for thiry-seven years. The Fir Domnan worshipped the god Domna. Domna was the father of Indech whose help was sought by Bres at the suggestion of Elatha, his father, when Bres lost his throne due to his lack of hospitality.

The Tuatha De Danann then invaded Ireland and defeated the Fir Bolg at the First Battle of Mag Tured. The victors allowed the Fir Bolg to keep the Province of Connacht, but some of them fled to the Islands of Arran, Islay, Rathlin, and Man. The Tuatha De Danann were those descendants of Nemed who had fled from the Formorians and had gone to the northern islands of the world to learn druidry, heathenism and devilish knowledge. There they became experts in every art and then returned to Ireland as the Tuatha De Danann. Such was the greatness of their knowledge, that they came without ships or vessels and lighted upon the mountain of Conmaicne Rein in Connachta.

How Provinces Came To Be

Five brothers then who were five kings
    Led subjects cross the sea.
They settled on the Emerald Isle
    And kingdoms came to be.

The first was called the race of Bolg,
    The second, the race of Damnann.
The third was called the Galion.
    All shared the land in common.

The men of Damnann had three kings,
    The others each had one.
Elected as their foremost king,
    Was Slane of Galion.

These kings divided Ireland
    In sections known as fifths,
Five provinces of gorgeous lands
    With valleys, hills, and cliffs.

Great Ulster north and Connacht west,
    And Meithe found in the middle.
Then Munster, Leinster, south and east,
    This solves the compass riddle.

Their rule upon this Irish soil
    Did not endure too long,
The tribe of goddess Danu came,
    And sang a battle song.

The Tuatha De Danann

The Irish word "Tuatha" means tribe. The Tuatha De Danann were the tribe of the goddess Danu, or "folks of the god whose mother is Dana." The Tuatha De Danann were descendants of Beothach, the son of Jarbonel, a son of Nemed. They were good gods in contra-distinction to the Formorians who were evil gods. The offspring of Jarbonel had learned wizardry and druidic teaching in the northern islands to which they had fled following the battle of Conann's Tower. Having learned the magical arts the descendants of Jarbonel returned to Ireland. The horse was now to follow the cart. Day was to follow night, light was to follow darkness, good gods were to replace the evil gods.

The Tuathans landed on the northeast coast of Ireland on the feast of Beltene, the first of May. Upon landing they demanded kingship or battle from the hated Fir Bolg. The Tuatha De Danann then defeated the Fir Bolg at the first battle of Mag Tured. They were victorious not by physical strength but by the magic which they had studied in the northern islands. The Tuatha de Danann were a tribe learned and wise and skilled in the arts of magic.

Some say the Tuatha De Danann came from the four great cities of heaven, Falia, Gorias, Finias, and Murias. It was said that they learned science and wisdom from the great sages enthroned in each of those cities. They were then wafted to Ireland on a magic cloud. When the cloud lifted, the Fir Bolg found them already encamped and fortified at Mag Tured.

They brought to Ireland with them four talismans: the Stone of Fal from Filias, which screamed when the rightful ruler of Ireland stepped on it; the Sword of Nuada from Gorias, whose wounds were always fatal; the Spear of Lug from Finias, which never missed its mark and always insured victory; and the Cauldron of Dagda, which came from Murias. No one ever partook from it without being satisfied. It is to these talismans that the Tuatha De Danann owe their supernatural power. They were gods because they were sorcerers and magicians.

Among the Tuatha De Danann only the artisans were considered gods (Dee). Only they knew the secrets of magic. The others were non-gods (Andee). The non-gods were the three sons of Bres, Brian, Iuchar, and Iucharba. We need to understand this distinction to understand the ancient Irish blessing: "May the blessing of the gods and non-gods be upon you."

The Fir Bolg sent Sreng to meet the enemy. The Tuatha De Danann sent Bres to meet the Fir Bolg. They examined each other's weapons. The spears of the Tuatha De Danann were light and sharply pointed. The spears of the Fir Bolg were heavy and blunt and dull. Science and brute force would now meet for the first time.

Fun with Irish Myths

The Fir Bolg refused compromise and decided to fight on the plains of Mag Tured. They were led by King Eochaid Mac Eirc. During the reign of Eochaid no rain fell in Ireland, only dew. There was no year without harvest. Spears disappeared from the land. Falsehood was banished from Ireland during his reign. Even though King Eochaid was a model king, he was the first king slain by weapons. The Fir Bolg had introduced kingship to Ireland in its sacred character. Eochaid Mac Eirc was the prototype of the just ruler. His wife was Tailtiu, lovely daughter of Mag Mor, king of Spain. After the death of Mac Eirc, Cecht asked Tailtiu to foster his son Lug whom he bore with Eithne, daughter of Balor.

The Fir Bolg were descendants of Umor (Big Eared), their ancestral deity. They were conquered by the Tuatha De Danann in the First Battle of Mag Tured, as were the Fir Damnann and the Galion. The Tuatha De Danann were led by Nuada, the Silver Hand. A hundred thousand were killed in this battle. It was in this battle that King Eochaid Mac Eirc was killed by the three sons of Nemed. After their defeat, the Fir Bolg were given the Province of Connacht under the protection of Medb and Ailill.

King Eochaid Mac Eirk

There was no king in all the land
　　More diligent at work,
Nor was a king more honest than
　　King Eochaid Mac Eirk.

The prototype of justice was
　　King Eochaid Mac Eirk.
Because he was so great a king,
　　The Fir Bolg had these perks.

While this king ruled the land was blessed
　　With harvest every year.
All lies were banished from the land,
　　And weapons disappeared.

And no rain fell in Ireland.
　　All water came from dew.
He was the very best of kings
　　The Irish ever knew.

This king was killed when gods appeared
　　Invading Ireland.
And he who was a man of peace,
　　Was slaughtered for his stand.

The Arrival of the
Tuatha De Danann

The tribes of goddess Danu came
    To Ireland from Northern Isles,
Where they had learned druidic truths,
    Which rivals thought were wiles.

They met the hated men of Bolg,
    And sought to be their king.
But Fir Bolg wanted none of this
    Tuatha badgering.

And so a battle then was fought
    In a Mag Tured field,
The Fir Bolg lost to magic,
    Which all Tuathas wield.

When these gods came to Irish shores,
    Four gifts they brought along.
And with these lucky talismans,
    These gods could do no wrong.

The first gift was the Stone of Fal,
    Proclaiming Irish king.
When rightful claimant stood on it,
    The stone went bellowing.

The second was Nuada's Sword,
    Which wounded like a shark.
The third gift was the Spear of Lug,
    Which never missed its mark.

The fourth charm was a cauldron,
    Which always fed its guest,
Who never left it hungry,
    Nor with its food depressed.

Tuatha were magician gods.
    Their magic made them blest.
The Fir Bolg never had a chance,
    As history will attest.

The Fir Bolg sent their warrior Sreng
    To meet Tuatha's Bres.
Bres urged that they divide the land,
    But Sreng would not say yes.

The war was now most imminent,
    So Lug was called to work,
To fight the men of Bolg led by
    King Eochaid Mac Eirc.

King Eochaid, the ideal king,
    Was perfect at his job.
And while he ruled, there were no coups,
    Nor rule by the mob.

Fun with Irish Myths

Nuada, called the Silver Hand,
    Led gods against mere men.
Hundred thousand Bolg were killed
    By Tuathan javelin.

And Eochaid, himself was killed,
    The first king killed by arms.
His followers surrendered then,
    Suppressed by magic charms.

So if you ever go to war
    Against the things divine,
Be smart enough to learn from Celts,
    To failure you're consigned.

Thus do not be some brainless nut,
    Who thinks himself supreme.
For when your actions worship self,
    You foolishly blaspheme.

You must be wise to face the facts.
    And humble you must be,
To see you're just a minnow in
    A universal sea.

Tuatha De Danann vs. Formorians

The Tuatha De Danann then came into conflict with the evil Formorians, the gods of the Fir Bolg, the Fir Damnann and the Fir Galion. This conflict came to a head in the Second Battle of Mag Tured. This was really a conflict between good and evil, between light and darkness, between order and disorder. Early in the war Nuada, king of the Tuatha De Danann, lost his arm in battle. Any disfiguration, any blemish, whether physical or moral, disqualified an Irish king as fit to rule. The mutilation of Nuada demanded his abdication and the selection of another king.

The Irish chieftains selected Bres (The Handsome) to replace Nuada as their king. Bres was the son of Elatha, a Formorian king. But although he himself was a Formorian, he had been raised by the Tuatha De Danann because his mother, Eri, was of that people. It soon became apparent that Bres had no leadership ability. The Formorians again held sway over the Tuatha De Danann. Bres taxed his subjects heavily and was inhospitable, a most serious crime in the mind of Irish Celts, a people most generous by nature. King Bres was thoroughly disliked by his chieftains because he lacked the Irish sense of generosity and the Irish spirit of genuine hospitality, which was the first and highest duty of any Irish king.

He provided neither poets nor jesters nor acrobats to entertain them. The poet Coirbre then uttered a satire against Bres. It was the first satire against an Irish king. These satires became rhythmic malediction by which poets could destroy a prince.

The chieftains demanded that Bres abdicate his kingship. Dian Cecht, The Leech, fitted Nuada with a silver arm. He was then reinstated as king. Bres sought the help of his Formorian father who gave him an army to retake his throne. Elatha suggested he seek the help of Balar and Indech, two chiefs of the Formorian gods. War was imminent. Lug who was the most celebrated of all Celtic gods then appeared on the scene to assist the Tuatha De Danann who were groaning under heavy Formorian oppression. Nuada relinquished his royal throne to Lug, that Lug might lead the Tuatha De Danann against the wicked Formorians. The Tuatha De Danann had five generals, their five chief gods: Dagda, Nuada, Ogma, Goibniu, and Dian Cecht.

Lug called the Tuatha De Danann to Council to take stock of their magical powers. He quickly organized the craftsmen, the sorcerers, the cup-bearers and the druids. The sorcerers promised to hurl the twelve mountains of Ireland against the enemy. The cup-bearers promised to drain all the lakes of Ireland. The druids promised three showers of fire on the Formorians to deprive them of two-thirds of their strength and to make it impossible for them or their horses to urinate.

During each battle Lug gave the Tuatha De Danann strength. He faced the one-eyed Balar, chief of the Formorian gods. Balar's eye was so large that it took four men to raise its lid. The venomous glance of Balar's eye could destroy an entire army. As soon as Balar opened his eye, Lug hurled a stone with a sling shot and drove that terrible eye to the back of his head so that it looked out at his own army destroying his own men as they glanced at it.

Balar, the god of night, was killed by Lug, the god of dawn. Balar's death routed the Formorians. A long time before his death, a druid had revealed to Balar that his own grandson would kill him. Balar was Lug's maternal grandfather. The story of Ethnea, Balar's daughter, is reminiscent of Danae in Greek mythology, whose son Perseus killed his grandfather as an oracle had predicted.

Tethra's sword fell into the hands of Ogma, the champion of the Tuatha De Danann. The sword spoke and related all the deeds it had done. Although the Formorians lost the sword of Tethra, they carried off the harp of Dagda. Lug and Ogma set off in pursuit of it. The Formorians were confident that they had succeeded in stealing the harp and hung it in their banquet hall. Lug and Ogma rushed in. The Dagda called for his harp and it left the wall and rush to him killing nine men on the way.

Fun with Irish Myths

The harp placed itself in the hands of the god who made beautiful music on it. He played three strains. These three strains always produced three effects. One strain produced tears and great weeping, another strain produced laughter, while a third strain produced sleep. As the Dagda began to play, there was at first great weeping among the Formorian women. He then played the second strain and the hall burst into laughter. He played the final strain and all fell asleep and the Tuatha De Danann left without injury to anyone.

During each battle Dian Cecht, The Leech, with his three children chanted incantations beside the well into which slain warriors were thrown. They immediately emerged restored to life and ready for further battle. With such magical powers the Tuatha De Danann easily won the war against the Formorians.

The War with the Formorians

Tuathas fought Formorians,
　　Who dwelt on Irish sod.
They conquered first the men of Bolg,
　　And then they fought their god.

Their king, Nuada, lost his arm,
　　And had to abdicate.
For any blemish in a king
　　Made that king second rate.

The Irish chiefs selected Bres
　　To take Nuada's place.
Bres then became Tuatha's king,
　　But couldn't reach first base.

He lacked that blessed Irish trait,
　　Called generosity.
He did not treat his chieftains well,
　　With reciprocity.

They bravely fought for him in war,
　　And never quit from fear.
But when they feasted in his house,
　　"Their breath smelled not of beer."

Nor were there bards or jesters there
　　To entertain his chiefs.
A malediction they pronounced,
　　That Bres would come to grief.

Fun with Irish Myths

An arm of silver then was made,
    By Dian Cecht, The Leech.
To fit Nuada's armless stub,
    So he again could reach.

The blemishes corrected now,
    Nuada could be king.
Bres then called on Formorian help
    For he was perishing.

The gods of dawn and gods of night
    Quite soon would be at war.
Tuatha and Formorians,
    Who'd be superior?

Tuathan gods would call on Lug,
    Their celebrated Lord.
Formorians called on Balar's help,
    Whom everyone abhorred.

Lug called for help from other gods,
    And asked what each could do.
They had a list of magic skills,
    That would assist his coup.

The Sorcerers would mountains hurl
    At the advancing foe.
Cup-bearers would drain all the lakes,
    Into which all streams flow.

The druids promised fire balls,
    Which all the world could see.
And then they promised something worse,
    No horse nor man could pee.

God Balar had a single eye,
    Large like a pyramid.
It was so large it truly took
    Four men to raise the lid.

With one glance from that evil eye,
    Whole troops could be destroyed.
So when you have such mighty help,
    Whom else need be employed?

Then Lug picked up a single stone,
    And hurled it at that eye.
And forcing it to rear of head
    Made all thing go awry.

The eye then gazed at his own men
    Those marching at his rear,
And as they glanced upon that eye,
    They quickly disappeared.

When Balar fell from mortal blow,
    Formorians were routed.
And when Tuathans saw his death,
    They all quite loudly shouted.

Fun with Irish Myths

How could Tuathans lose a war,
　　With Dian Cecht, the leech?
By incantations for the dead,
　　Each death the leech impeached.

I'm sure we all have wars to fight,
　　And need another's aid.
No man is self-sufficient, then,
　　In any escapade.

There always is some evil eye,
　　Which stares at each of us.
A Balar in some other guise,
　　Which is anonymous.

We need the help of Lug, I'm sure.
　　But we must ask for it.
Available from many friends,
　　But not the hypocrite.

So find yourself a real friend,
　　That you can always trust.
And when a crisis does arise,
　　You'll leave it in the dust.

The myths of ancient Irishmen
　　Can make us very wise,
If we but grasp their subtleties,
　　So often well disguised.

Dagda's Harp

The harp of Dagda was unique,
    It came on his command.
It came whenever he would call,
    And jumped into his hand.

This instrument had three effects
    When Dagda plucked its string.
The first effect on those who heard,
    Were tears that it would bring.

Then all who heard its melody
    would weep and loudly wail.
And as he played, it sounded like
    A mournful nightingale.

Then Dagda plucked a second strand,
    And laughter filled the hall.
It seemed like those who were on hand,
    All had a real ball.

But when the final strand was plucked,
    All present fell asleep.
A brilliant way to catch a nap!
    It sure beats counting sheep.

Though none of us has such a harp,
    Its pattern we repeat.
At first we think that all our life
    Is filled with bitter-sweet.

Fun with Irish Myths

And so we weep and wail a lot.
    We think life is the pits.
Until we grow in wisdom's school,
    And find that each piece fits.

Then laughter follows weeping,
    And we enjoy life more.
We understand its subtleties
    And what they hold in store.

We find life now more joyful,
    Our friends a treasured gem.
For trash we thought important once,
    We sing a requiem.

Then after all life's laughter,
    We finally fall asleep.
And underneath the rug of death,
    The cares we had we sweep.

This is the Irish way of life,
    At least for those I know.
I think their way superlative.
    It is the way to go.

Perhaps that's why they smile so much,
    And live life to the hilt.
That's why they're such a happy bunch,
    It's how their race is built.

So Irish problem solving then,
    Must never be "forgot."
It really is quite simple!
    Just cry and laugh a lot.

The Rule of the Tuatha De Danann

Formorians were finally expelled from Ireland forever. They returned to their own country, the land of the dead, where souls find a new body and a second dwelling place. Tethra rules there as the god of the dead. Once the Formorians were expelled, the island became the exclusive domain of the Tuatha De Danann. Bres, the traitor, was captured. He bargained for his life by promising the cattle of Ireland would always be in milk and there would be a harvest each quarter. The Tuatha rejected his promises but spared his life in exchange for advice on the proper time of plowing, sowing, and reaping. These were the secrets the Tuatha De Danann needed to know to become an agricultural people.

After the second battle of Mag Tured, Tuathans ruled Ireland until the coming of the Milesians. Tuathans represented the Celtic reverence for knowledge, art, and poetry. As gods of light, they conquered the Fir Bolg, the symbol of dullness and the Formorians, the symbol of darkness.

The age of the Tuatha De Danann depicts a fairytale view of morality. It was not a matter of good or evil. They were unaware of such concepts. They were only aware of pleasure and suffering. This was the good or evil they knew. This was the only morality prevalent among the Tuathan gods and Irish mortals in Celtic myths.

After the Formorians

Old Tethra, the Formorian god,
  Now governs the land of death,
Where all Formorian souls find,
  New bodies and new breath.

In Ireland they live no more,
  Expelled there long ago.
No longer will they breathe its air
  Nor see its shamrocks grow.

Tuathan gods replaced them there,
  And dwelled there long in peace.
They learned to farm those fertile lands,
  Which from the kings they'd lease.

They ruled this land of Ireland,
  'Til came the Sons of Mil
And if Milesians had not come,
  Those gods would rule it still.

They had a love and reverence
  For knowledge and for art,
Especially for poetry,
  Which played a noble part.

The Irish were illiterate.
  All writing was forbidden.
But they were far more scholarly,
  Than scholars that had written.

Druidic law forbid them write,
    Lest mysteries be revealed.
So things were passed on orally,
    And still were kept quite sealed.

Their tales of former glory days,
    Were orally handed down.
In poetry of every kind,
    Which wore a special crown.

The Celts then shined a special light,
    Which Caesar never knew.
He thought Celts should be Roman-like,
    In everything they do.

His judgment was but prejudice,
    Which kept him ignorant,
Of other lights and grandeur,
    Because they're different.

We might think morals missing there,
    In Irish bygone days.
They'd not condemn what we'd condemn,
    Nor praise what we would praise.

They had no knowledge of the good,
    Which we'd today maintain.
Their knowledge was like Pavlov's dog,
    Of pleasure and of pain.

Fun with Irish Myths

Because they love their golden past,
    And think the present trite,
We sometimes think the Irish are,
    Quite prejudiced from fright.

But if we see through clearer eyes,
    Then something else is cast.
For due to temporality,
    The present will be past.

So do not be too much impressed,
    With what's now going on,
Especially if it's second rate,
    An unimportant pawn.

And do not be so stupid as
    To denigrate the past,
Unless you know its history,
    And why it didn't last.

Because a thing is popular,
    In any culture now,
Is not an invitation that
    It stand and take a bow.

Look rather at the culture then,
    That holds it in esteem.
Perhaps it is a culture that
    Itself ran out of steam.

The Sons of Mil

After the Tuatha De Danann ruled Ireland for one hundred and sixty-nine years, the Sons of Mil arrived there on May 1, 516 B.C. Mil was the son of Bile, the god of death. The word "Mil" is derived from Mil Espane — Spanish Soldier. These Goidels lived in Scythia originally. They were descendants of Fairsaid and Goidel Glas. According to ancient legends, Fenius was exiled from Egypt. He wandered through Africa for forty-two years. At last he came to the Column of Hercules, crossed to Spain and settled there. Scota was Mil's wife. There are three names for these ancient Irish, Fenius, Scota, and Goidel, which means a son of Scota.

The Goidels set out for Ireland after Ith, Mil's uncle, and saw its shores from a tower built by Bregnon, the grandfather of Mil. In those days Ireland was ruled by three kings, the grandsons of Dagda: Mac Cuill, married to the goddess Banba; Mac Cecht, married to the goddess Fotla; and Mac Green, married to the goddess Eire. When Ith landed the kings were meeting at Ailech in Donegal to divide the inheritance of Neit, the god of war, who had been killed by the Formorians. When they returned home the kings murdered Ith, who was taken back to Spain. The Sons of Mil considered this murder an act of war and invaded Ireland to overthrow the Tuathans. The race of men were now at war with the race of gods. The Irish had now arrived on Irish soil.

The Race of Men

The Irish of the present day
    Came from the land of Spain,
Five hundred years before Our Lord.
    Now please let me explain.

They came to Spain from Egypt's realm,
    From which they'd been exiled.
They traversed darkest Africa,
    Cross rivers crocodiled.

They crossed the Columns of Hercules,
    And thus arrived in Spain,
The first who did discover it
    Rains mainly on the plain.

Atop a lofty tower there,
    Erin was seen by Ith,
The uncle of a man named Mil.
    My source is Irish myth.

Uncle Ith then sailed away,
    Perhaps, within the hour,
To travel to the far off land
    That he had seen from tower.

When he set foot on Irish soil,
    No one was there for greeting,
For all the kings of Ireland
    Had gone off to a meeting.

Fun with Irish Myths

The grandsons of the Dagda were
    The kings who ruled this land,
Mac Cuill, Mac Cecht, besides Mac Green,
    Each with his own command.

When they returned and found Ith there,
    They could not be much ruder.
They quickly killed the guest from Spain
    Whom they thought an intruder.

These kings were wed to goddesses,
    Well-known in Irish query.
All served as Irish epithets
    Fotla, Banba, and Eire.

These goddesses would later play
    A most prophetic role,
As they foretold forthcoming days
    And who'd be in control.

The Invasion of the Sons of Mil

When the body of Ith was brought back to Spain by his companions, thirty-six chiefs of the race of Mil quickly set out to avenge his death. Each chief had his own ship, his own family, and his own men. The poet Amairgin was the scholar of the fleet. His wife died while on the long journey. The fleet landed on the first of May, the feast of Beltene, the god of death. When they set foot on Irish soil Amairgin offered prayers for the help of this land and the help of nature against the gods. He sought to overcome the Tuatha De Danann by "File" or knowledge instead of violence. He called upon science and the forces of nature to defeat the gods.

No sooner did these Goidels land than they were confronted by the Tuatha De Danann, the local gods. The first three inhabitants of Ireland that the Sons of Mil met on their arrival were the three goddesses of that land, Eire, Banba, and Fotla. The goddess Eire predicted that the land of Ireland would belong to the descendants of the Sons of Mil forever.

Amairgin, the wise poet of the Sons of Mil, thanked her reverently. But Donn, the oldest of the Sons of Mil, said to her rather rudely: "It is not you we must thank, but our own gods and our own magic powers." Eire replied: "What is that to you, for neither you nor your children will enjoy this land." The goddess Eire then asked Amairgin that the Island bear her name forever. Her sisters made the same request. Thus, the island has three names, Eire, Banba, and Fotla, Ireland's three original goddesses.

The goddess Eire's prophesy came true. Donn who had offended her so irreverently was drowned with his three children even before he found a home. He was buried on an island off the west coast of Ireland which still bears his name. The island is still called the House of Donn. After their deaths the Sons of Mil join him there where he is known as Lord of the dead. The scholarly poet Amairgin, through his wisdom, secured possession of the country for his race by conciliating its ancient goddesses. In his ignorance Donn failed to reside peacefully in this new land because he rejected its local cults and invoked other gods.

Vengeance of the Sons of Mil

The ancient kings of Ireland
    Abused their Spanish guest.
For when he came to pay a call,
    He found himself hard-pressed.

Instead of welcoming a friend,
    They slew him as a foe.
Instead of hospitality,
    They dealt a deadly blow.

When Ith was carried back to Spain,
    Revenge was quickly planned.
The leaders of the Sons of Mil,
    Would soon invade that land.

They anchored boats on Beltene's feast,
    And opted to explore.
They met the local goddesses,
    When first they stepped ashore.

Wise Eire then revealed to them,
    They'd always rule this land.
Amairgin politely thanked her,
    But Donn found reprimand.

When Donn refused to reverence her,
    The goddess prophesied,
Not he nor any progeny,
    Would on her land abide.

Her prophesy was verified,
    As Donn was forthwith drowned,
Then brought to some off-island site
    And buried in the ground.

The goddess Eire then besought
    A favor from the poet,
She asked the island bear her name,
    And that's how we still know it.

There's quite a difference one can find,
    'Tween poet and the fighter,
Amairgin and the soldier Donn,
    The calm and the igniter.

The varied actions of these men,
    A prudent lesson "brung" them,
For when you make too many waves
    You'll soon be placed among them.

The poet chose the wiser part,
    And gathered his reward.
He catered to the god's request,
    As history does record.

He still is praised by Irishmen,
    These many centuries later.
He's called a gentle man of peace,
    But Donn an agitator.

Fun with Irish Myths

And every Irishman since then,
    Will be one of these two.
He'll demonstrate his gentle charm,
    Or he will clobber you.

The Irish temper is controlled
    Most often by that race.
But when it's lost we must watch out,
    And give it breathing-space.

In dealing with the Irish, then,
    Just keep a careful eye.
And know that you are dealing with
    A race of Gemini.

The Sons of Mil Meet
the Tuatha De Danann

The Sons of Mil arrived at Tara, the capital of ancient Ireland. Mac Cuill, Mac Cecht, and Mac Green, the three kings of Ireland, were there. The Sons of Mil demanded they surrender. The kings requested time to think it over. In the meantime, they had their Tuathan druids concocting enchantments to drive the invaders out. Mac Cuill finally agreed to accept the judgment of Amairgin. Poets, not kings nor politicians, were the arbitrators for the ancient Irish.

Amairgin called upon the Sons of Mil to withdraw to the ninth wave. Tuathan druids then invoked magic to cause storms to scatter the ships of the Sons of Mil. Their druidic winds blew but no higher than the ship's mast. The scholarly Amairgin counteracted the magic of the Tuatha De Danann by calling upon nature and its laws. The ships of the Sons of Mil then landed again on Irish shores.

The Sons of Mil gave battle to the Tuatha De Danann at Tailtiu and killed a great number of them. Math, the son of Umor, was the druid for the Tuatha De Danann. It was he who introduced shouting and uproar and noise of every kind as a means of frightening the enemy in battle. The Tuatha De Danann concocted three demonic shouts to confuse

87

and bewilder their enemy — whistling, weeping, and lamentation.

The three kings of the Tuatha De Danann were slain in battle and the three goddesses were dispersed. When peace was restored, Amairgin divided the land into equal parts. The lower half, the part under the earth, was given to the Tuatha De Danann. They hid and became invisible and took up residence in caves and underground mounds where they still dwell. The Sons of Mil were given the upper half, the surface of the earth.

Even though the Tuathan gods were vanquished, they still controlled the fertility of the earth and so their power was considerable. Whenever they wished they could deprive the Sons of Mil of milk and harvest. Their underground home of caves and mounds is called the kingdom of the sid. Those who dwell there are called sid-folk, fairy-folk, or goblin hosts.

The Sons of Mil in Ireland

The sons of Mil in Ireland,
    Were not believed divine.
But all who came before them there,
    Were gods by Celt's design.

They came to Erin to avenge,
    The cruel death of Ith.
The story of their sojourn is
    The core of Irish myth.

They marched to Tara and to war
    Against Tuathan kings.
They fought against the magic of
    Druidic banterings.

Great numbers of those ancient gods
    Were killed by Sons of Mil.
They hid in mounds and rocky caves,
    It's there that they are still.

So if you visit Ireland,
    And see things unexplained.
It's just Tuathans from the mounds,
    As has been fore-ordained.

These people play a foremost part,
    In tales that Irish tell.
In every Irish happening,
    They somehow cast their spell.

The World of the Sid

Following the division of the earth by the poet Amairgin in which the Sons of Mil were to occupy the surface of the earth and the Tuatha De Danann were to occupy the underground world of mounds and caves, the Dagda divided this underworld among the Tuatha De Danann into divisions called sids. Each god had his own sid or kingdom. There was a sid for Lug, a sid for Ogma, a sid for every god, while the Dagda kept two sids for himself. There were sids beneath deep waters and unknown islands over which Mananann and Tethra held sway. Anything that was outside the circle lit by the fires of men belonged to the people of the sid, the otherworld folk of Ireland.

The otherworld people of the sid frequently fought among themselves. In those skirmishes they often times sought the help of human heroes or kings. In exchange for the services sought they offered the love of a fairy mistress in return. They felt it was a generous and gracious reward.

The people of the sid were eternally young and thus immortal. They often died, however, which is a part of the many inconsistencies so frequently found in Irish mythology. The sid folk were mortal only by accident. They were subject to bodily wounds, but their world was not subject to time. It was only when they left the world of the sid that time caught up with them. And just as time was foreign to the world of the sid, so also was space. A whole tribe of otherworld people could dwell in a single modest mound. All their dwellings and lands and all their possessions could be contained within the smallest mound.

The sid was primarily a place of feasting. Each sid had its banquet hall (Bruiden). And each and every Bruiden had its Dagda's cauldron which was always full. The Lord of the otherworld feast was always represented as a man carrying a pig, for pork was the Irishman's first love. In the "Bruiden" feast a pig was killed each day and that same pig always lived tomorrow. The Bruiden was the Celtic Valhalla. The cauldron was always full of the food of one's choice.

Long ago the Tuatha De Danann withdrew from the surface of the earth to reside in their many underground palaces in the world of the sid. They have been vanquished by the Sons of Mil. Gods have been vanquished by men. Still those gods are immortal. They still appear from time to time and still exercise considerable power in the world of mortals. At times that power is beneficial; at times it is not. When the people of the sid appear in the world of humans, they most often appear as animals or birds. They sometimes, however, appear as men.

There are two races now that inhabit Ireland. The one is imperishable, the Tuatha De Danann. The other is perishable and subject to decay and death, the Sons of Mil. The historical record of the

Fun with Irish Myths

Sons of Mil in Ireland centers around the life of heroes in the service of the kings of Ulster. This part of Irish mythology is called the Ulster cycle. It is far less magical than the Mythological cycle just discussed.

The World of the Otherworld

Tuathan gods had lost the war
    And hid beneath the ground,
Amarigin had consigned them there
    To roam each cave and mound.

Then Dagda who was chief of gods,
    Divided up this realm,
Into divisions called a sid
    With some god at each helm.

And any place that can be found
    Beyond the fires of men,
Belongs to these Tuathan gods,
    Who died and live again.

They sometimes lure the Sons of Mil,
    The humans of this land,
To palaces beneath the earth
    By fairy mistress hand.

The people of the otherworld
    Eternally are young.
But life outside the world of men
    So often goes unsung.

All life within the world of Sid,
    Converges on the feast.
They have there all they want to eat,
    A pig a day, at least.

Fun with Irish Myths

Pork is the favorite Irish food.
    All else is second best.
When pork is placed before them,
    The Irish are obsessed.

But what about potatoes, then?
    Aren't they the Irish prize?
That's potato grower's blarney
    Which farmers advertise!

At all their feasts they have their ale,
    And drink and boast a lot.
The Celt loves to exaggerate,
    In case you have "forgot."

Some think the Celt is telling lies,
    When he expands his tale.
It's just exaggeration, though,
    Which grows with too much ale!

At every feast there is a fight,
    Resulting from this dig?
"Who is the strongest man that's here?
    For he will carve the pig."

Though said in jest, I think it's true,
    Dissensions you will find,
When mingling much with Irishmen,
    Unless you're really blind.

Dagda, King of Sid

The Dagda was to Irish myths
    What Zeus was to the Greek.
The sid was his Olympic home,
    Where gods played hide and seek.

The trees that grew within the sid
    Were laden with much fruit.
And ale was always there on hand,
    Which no one could dilute.

Two pigs were kept in every sid,
    One living and one roasting.
And no one ever thought of death.
    It's life the sid was toasting.

The Dagda and his wife Boann,
    Were parents to a son.
They raised him in this otherworld,
    Where Oengus had much fun.

Then Oengus saw a pretty maid,
    While dreaming every night.
He fell so much in love with her,
    He lost his appetite.

He couldn't eat, he grew quite ill.
    His parents were distressed.
They sought his love throughout the land,
    In vain, I might suggest.

Fun with Irish Myths

King Bodb was Munster's clever king,
    And known to be quite wise.
Boann quite humbly sought his help,
    And he soon found the prize.

'Twas at the Lake of Dragon's Mouth,
    That Bodb had seen the maiden.
So Oengus journeyed to that lake,
    Where lots of maids were wadin'.

But every maid gave way to one,
    As milk gives way to cream.
Her name was Caer from Connaught town,
    The woman of his dream.

The Dagda went to King Ailill,
    Requesting he assist,
By going to Caer's father, and
    For daughter's hand insist.

Caer's father, Ethal, told Ailill,
    His daughter was a con.
One year she'd be a lovely girl,
    The next she'd be a swan.

The change was on November first,
    On Samhain's feast each year.
So Oengus was on hand that day
    To see the swan appear.

He called to her his tender love
    with hopes she would concur.
He'd like to be a lovely swan,
    And swim about with her.

The two returned to Dagda's sid,
    And led a swan-like life.
There Caer and Oengus swam about,
    And she became his wife.

This teaches us a lesson then
    That each of us should learn.
Don't make decisions half asleep,
    Or often you'll get burned.

You must be very careful of
    The girl of your dreams,
For it could often happen that
    She's not all that she seems.

What you in sleep think lovely
    Might really be a goose,
Or it might be a gull or swan,
    Or god forbid, a moose.

So pick your mate while you're awake,
    And not while half asleep.
Or you could rashly waste your life,
    By swimming in the deep.

Fun with Irish Myths

So don't behave like Oengus did
    And be confused by dreams.
For what you think the real world,
    "Ain't" really what it seems.

So dreams are dreams but only dreams,
    And not what you might wish.
When you awake you find dream's pledge
    Was only gibberish.

So realize the dreams you dream
    Are simply just a token,
A symbol of some gorgeous swan,
    But swans are not house broken.

As you awake and realize
    You've heard a swan song sung,
You know at least that you're not stuck
    With all that gone swan's dung.

The Celtic New Year

The Tuatha De Danann and the Sons of Mil were the two races that shared the Emerald Isle. Each race had equal rights and equal dignity. For the most part, the two races maintained friendly relations with one another. They respected each other's world and seldom trespassed the other's domain, except on the unique night of Samhain. On the night of Samhain that which separated the two worlds was withdrawn and the two worlds were in communication with one another. This was the Celtic New Year.

The Celtic calendar was not regulated by the solar year. Their year was agrarian and pastoral. It was based on harvesting and planting, not on the movement of the sun. Their goddesses were goddesses of the earth. The Irish year began with the feast of Samhain, November first. The half year was celebrated on the feast of Beltene, May first. The year was also split into quarters, or half of the half. The feast of Imbolg was February first, the beginning of the first quarter, or half of the first half. The feast of Lugnasad was August first, the beginning of the third quarter, or half of the second half.

Samhain was not a feast of any tutelary deity, but a feast of the whole world of the spirits, who on this night intruded into the world of men. On this night whole troops of otherworld people came from the sid and attacked the dwellings of men. Fires and drownings were common on this night. A carry over of this incendiary practice can still be seen today in certain cities of our own country, like Detroit, in which burnings have become commonplace on this evening recalling the ancient Celtic feast of Sam-hain.

On this night tithes and sacrifices were offered to the spirits, not as offerings to guardian powers, but as a tribute to their powers of destruction. The race of Nemed sacrificed grain and even children to the cruel Formorian gods at Cromm Cruach in bloody rites based upon terror. The Teutates were pacified by drownings. Taranis was propitiated by burnings. Other gods were appeased by hangings. Events such as these were recalled on the feast of Samhain. It was a night of chaos. A world that was normally closed to men was abruptly opened to them.

In an effort to undo the chaos which centered around the worship of the false gods of paganism and to focus man's attention on the harmony which results from the worship of the true God, the Church made this feast of Samhain the universal feast of All Saints. Rather than trying to fight an established feast, the Church merely gave man a more sacred reason for celebrating it.

The Celtic Calendar

The Celtics cut the year in half,
    And then each half in two.
They ended up with quarters then,
    And four were not too few.

The calendar controlled their lives,
    In planting or in battle,
In everything they did or touched,
    Their lambings and their cattle.

The druids regulated it,
    And this way they held sway.
They were the judges and the priests,
    That none dared disobey.

Their Samhain was November first,
    The first day of the year.
And as this feast day came around,
    All mortals lived in fear.

For on that day the spirit world
    Walked in the world of men.
And many evil, magic things
    Their presence did portend.

The dark half of the Celtic year
    Again was split in two.
Beginning with the Imbolg feast,
    Spring made its rendezvous.

Fun with Irish Myths

This feast was February first
    It honored goddess Bridgit.
Since she was patroness of births,
    Celts welcomed lamb and piglet.

This goddess of prosperity,
    Brought gifts to Irish homes.
The footprints seen within their hearths,
    Were made as Bridgit roamed.

Saint Bridgit then eventually,
    This pagan god replaced,
As spreading Christianity
    all pagan cults erased.

The feast of Beltene was May first.
    The word means "Fire of Bel."
It introduced bright summer days,
    Which bid the cold farewell.

And Lugnasad was August first,
    Observed by every Celt,
In honor of a god named Lug,
    To which all Irish knelt.

It was a feast of harvesting,
    Much like our country fair.
Observed almost religiously
    By Irish everywhere.

Fun with Irish Myths

Perhaps we think past Irishmen
    Bore superstition's scars.
But what about those folks today,
    Who guide their lives by stars.

They base life on the zodiac
    And sundry other things.
The sorcerer and wizard thrive
    And cons become their kings.

I think we are more gullible,
    Than Irish ever were.
So many things so clear to them,
    To us are just a blur.

They knew exactly why they lived,
    And were a happy lot.
They understood the joys of life
    Without the need of pot.

So pity not past Irishmen,
    Who lived so long ago.
It's they who'd pity us today,
    For what we've got to show.

The Druids

"Druid" means knowledge of the oak. The oak was sacred to the Celt. It was an object of worship. Druids were common to Celts in every part of the world. They were a privileged class, exempt from taxes and military service. They served as teachers, judges, and priests. They were intermediaries between the tribe and the tribal gods. Considered men of wisdom, they were treated by all with a dignity equal to kings.

Above all druids was one arch-druid. Druidic training was rigorous and took nearly twenty years to accomplish. Druids had to memorize vast amounts of oral learning. They memorized laws, rituals, genealogies and tribal histories. In this way Irish folktales were handed down from one generation to the next until Christian monks committed them to writing centuries later.

A chief function of the druid was to preside at human sacrifices. The Romans spoke of these Celtic sacrifices with disgust. Altars were drenched with the blood of prisoners. Druids consulted the entrails of victims to know the will of their gods. Pliny said with disgust: "To kill a man was the highest religious function and to eat him was even more salubrious." The Romans hated druids perhaps more for political reasons than for religious ones, for druids united the Celts against Roman advancements.

The Sacred Caste

Celts had a class of sacred men,
Druids, bards, and poets.
Whose duty was to guard their truth,
So future Celts would know it.

They served as judges in their courts,
Promoting common good.
They were revered by every class,
An honored brotherhood.

They interceded with the gods,
And offered sacrifice.
And when the tribes engaged in wars,
Both sides sought their advice.

The mistletoe that grew on oaks,
Had special healing might,
If cut by golden sickles manned
By druids dressed in white.

And to preserve their privileged rank,
They kept their magic hidden.
Vast knowledge then was memorized,
For writing was forbidden.

For twenty years they went to school
To learn druidic lore
This later served apprenticeship,
For Europe's troubadour.

The Hero

Irish myths are among the world's oldest recorded stories. Irish are born storytellers. There are four groups of early Irish myths. Each group is called a cycle. First, there is the Mythological cycle which contains stories about the otherworld people. Secondly, there is the Ulster cycle which contains tales about the exploits of Ulstermen some four hundred years before Christ. Thirdly, there is the cycle of Kings. At this point Irish myths enter the realm of real historical kings, and not just the realm of euhemerized gods. Finally, there is the Find or Ossianic cycle which deals with the adventures of Find Mac Cumaill and his son Ossin.

Celtic mythology suffers from euhemerism which treats ancient gods merely as ancient heroes. This is due in part to the efforts of the Irish monks who retold these stories centuries later and tried to purge them of all reference to their pagan context. In spite of these efforts, there is a kind of unique naturalness in which the ancient Irish passed in and out of the natural and the supernatural. They had no real difficulties with the supernatural order.

There is a kind of orderliness in Irish mythology. All gods are beautiful. There is nothing to cause alarm or opposition. There is no sin, no punishment, few monsters, no extremes, no serious wars, no lasting strife. Those who die are taken to a land of promise and attain an ideal existence of beauty and youth.

The Celtic world was populated with many supernatural beings who co-ruled the earth with man. Man originally won his freedom from these otherworld beings, sometimes by force and sometimes by magic. These two inhabitants of the earth, men and gods, are rival powers. At times they are friendly. At times they are hostile. It is into such a world that the Irish hero is born.

The hero was a mythological figure, human in every way, but not beyond the incarnation of ideal qualities. It was in the hero that Celts sought to make incarnate the ideal qualities of their race. The hero was not a god. He belonged to the world of men. Spirits, elves, fairies, and gods belonged to the world of the sid. The hero belonged to this world. He was a descendant of the Sons of Mil.

"Nia" is the Celtic word for hero. It is also the word for combat. The hero overflowed with life and energy, combat and excitement. The hero was described in words expressing fury, ardor, speed and a blazing energy that consumed him. Cu Chulaind, the hero par excellence, personified heroic fury.

The hero was the defender and champion of his people. He was not their ancestor. Heroes died without posterity. He was the ideal youth, a fighter for the glory of the tribe. A hero was expected to protect his people from enemies and enrich them by raids. The hero had many foster parents for he belonged to the whole community. Thus we see in the story of Setantae or Cu Chulaind that Amairgin reared him; Sencha taught him wisdom; Fergus taught him to use weapons; and Cathbad, the druid, instructed him in magic.

The hero always bore a kind of stigmata. Cu Chulaind possessed this hero's moon. In the height of battle he possessed the hero's fury. So violent was that fury that he had to be plunged three times into vats of cold water to calm him down.

Marriage was an important part of the hero's life. The Irish insisted that their heroes marry. The hero needed a wife so that he would leave other men's wives alone. A hero's training began in the tribe and was completed in the royal court. He was instructed in the jargon of poets and knew kennings, riddles and wisdom. Heroes always possessed "gessa," things they must or may not do. The more important the hero the more gessa he had — Cu Chulaind had nineteen. If the hero defiled his gessa he was defenseless before the enemy. Sometimes the gessa was contradictory as was the case with Cu Chulaind.

The final mark of the hero was a violent death. The constant problem of Celtic mythology was to justify the death of a hero with his strength and invincibility. All heroic stories faced the same dilemma. To solve this problem the hero's death was always seen as the unfair result of deception and not the result of any weakness. Roland was betrayed by Ganelon;

Achilles was struck from behind; Cu Chulaind was victimized by his contradictory gessa. One gessa stated that he could not pass by a hearth without tasting its food, while another gessa forbade him taste the flesh of dogs. He was a victim of his gessa as he passed by the hearth where the children of Calatin were cooking a dog.

Ireland's greatest hero was Cu Chulaind. He was to the Irish what Hercules was to the Greeks. He was the hero above all others. His name was Setantae. He was the typical mythical hero, human to the extreme, yet the incarnation of ideal qualities. His birth was supernatural.

Conchubur was king of Ulster. His sister, Deichtine, was his charioteer. One day while on a chase near Brug na Boinne, the most famous fairy dwelling place in Ireland and home of the Dagda, Conchubur and his troops were overtaken by nightfall. He sent two warriors in search of lodging. They found a little house inhabited by a man and his wife, but they had no food. The house soon became large enough to house the whole troop of warriors and supply them with an abundance of food and ale.

During the night the woman of the house gave birth to a child and a mare gave birth to two foals which Deichtine gave as a gift to the newly born infant. When morning came, everything had disappeared. There was no house, no couple, only the child and the two colts. A man approached Deichtine. It was the god Lug. He informed her that it was

he who brought her to the sid and she would soon
bear his son.

The men of Ulster did not understand such a
mysterious birth. They accused the king in his
drunkenness of begetting a child on his own sister.
Conchubur then betrothed Deichtine to the warrior
Sualtaim in an effort to silence the vicious rumors.
She eventually gave birth to the god Lug's child and
named him Setantae.

Cu Chulaind, Hero of the Ulaid

Who was the greatest Irishman
 By destiny ordained?
The son of Lug, the greatest god,
 Setantae, Cu Chulaind!

We'll tell the story of his birth,
 And how he came to be,
And how he reached that great renown,
 Which was his destiny.

King Conchubur was Ulaid's chief.
 His sister was Deichtine.
She also was his charioteer,
 But not his concubine.

One time when they were on a chase,
 At nightfall they sought shelter.
Then Lug appeared and wooed Deichtine,
 And pregnancy he dealt her.

Who was the father of her child?
 The Ulaid sought to know.
Was father other than the king?
 And if he were, how so?

They didn't know that Lug dropped by,
 Just seeking Deichtine's love.
Nor did they know the son begot,
 Was caused by god above.

Fun with Irish Myths

Then king betrothed his sister to
    Sualtaim, Roech's son,
That talk of lust and incest,
    Might thereby be undone.

So learn the lesson myths teach us
    Don't rashly judge your neighbor.
For what you judge the work of man
    Could be some godly labor.

The crosses we are given, then,
    Don't always seem a blessing.
Unless we see behind the scenes,
    They could seem most oppressing.

The Irish know that they possess
    Most faults they see in others.
So gossip's not a common trait
    Kids learn from Irish mothers.

I'm sure the Irish that I know,
    Put rumors on a shelf.
For what they'd spread of others,
    They'd have to spread of self.

Most Irish know the weaknesses
    And foibles they possess.
And thus they know what they'd condemn,
    They too must soon confess.

Cu Chulaind as a Boy

When Deichtine gave birth to Setantae, Amairgin was asked to rear him. Fergus taught him weaponry and the druid Cathbad taught him the art of magic. At a very early age he was sent to Conchubur at Emuin Machae to be reared with the one hundred and fifty boys raised there in the palace of the king. Even as a child of seven, he excelled in play and in sports and displayed that insolent excess, or defiance of fate, so necessary to the Celtic hero. The other boys at once rejected him and hurled their javelins at him, but he warded each of them off with his toy shield.

It was at this time that Setantae first received his "riastarthae" or hero's fury, a special mark or character visibly borne by Celtic heroes. His mouth opened so wide that his guts could be seen. One eye sunk into his skull and shrank to the size of a pinpoint. The other eye protruded onto his cheek and became as large as a bowl. A hero's moon appeared on his forehead. In this fury he defeated all the other boys together. They were then placed under his protection, rather than he under theirs.

At another time while Setantae was taking a nap the Ulaid were attacked and badly defeated by Eogan son of Durthacht. The cries of the survivors soon awakened him. He arose and set out for the field of battle where he searched for Conchubur.

Fun with Irish Myths

When a ghost tried to detain him he struck off its head. He finally found Conchubur in a ditch and lifted him out which six champion warriors could not have done. He took his king to a nearby house, lit a fire and bathed his wounds. Conchubur asked for a roasted pig that he might live. Cu Chulaind set out in search of it and soon found a man roasting a pig over a spit in the middle of the forest. He took the man's pig and the man's head.

After the king had eaten the pig, Cu Chulaind took him home. On the way home they came upon Cuscraid, the son of Conchubur. He also was seriously wounded. The boy, Cu Chulaind, carried both of them back to Emuin Machae.

These and many other unbelievable accomplishments of Cu Chulaind as a child have been handed down by word of mouth over many centuries. The Irish truly loved their heroes, and even though their exploits could not be written down because of druidic law, they were handed down orally from one generation to the next so that their heroic deeds would never be forgotten.

Cu Chulaind as a Child

Cu Chulaind was the Hercules
    Of Irish history.
His feats and deeds and magic skills
    Are filled with mystery.

When he was just a lad of six,
    He stunned the royal court.
While playing with three fifty boys,
    He won at every sport.

And even at this early age
    "Riastarthae" appeared.
The special warrior's fury mark,
    That indicates career.

One eye recedes into the skull,
    The other eye protrudes,
And forehead's marked by hero's moon,
    All signs of fortitude.

Chief Conall Cernach fostered him.
    Amairgin was his guide.
Brave Fergus taught him weaponry.
    Which uncle did provide.

So if one eye is hanging out,
    And laying on your face,
Don't think you're called like Cu Chulaind,
    To save the Irish race.

Fun with Irish Myths

For I have seen some Irishmen,
    Who looked just like I've said.
But it was in a bar brawl fight,
    Where each had lost his head.

Or if your mouth is opened wide,
    So others see your gut,
Don't think that you can beat the world,
    Or it will beat your butt.

Or if a moon somehow appears
    On forehead quite pronounced,
Don't try to take the whole world on,
    Or surely you'll get trounced.

I'm sure that many Irishmen
    Feel called to play the hero,
Especially after several beers
    Reduced their brains to zero.

And so their wives must watch with care,
    For every Irish quirk.
An Irishman in any bar
    Will make himself a jerk.

Why Setantae's Name Was Changed

Why was Setantae called "Cu Chulaind" or "Hound of Culann?" It happened when Culann invited Conchubur to a feast. The king asked his nephew to accompany him. The child said he would follow later. Not knowing this, Culann closed the gates and put his watchdog in the courtyard to guard his home and his cattle. This hound was so vicious that it required nine men with three chains to hold him. All had forgotten that Setantae was still to come.

As the boy journeyed along he hurled his toy javelin and raced to catch it before it hit the ground. When he entered the courtyard the wicked dog attacked. The lad killed the dog with his bare hands breaking every bone in its body. All were amazed at his strength and courage.

Culann was happy that the lad was unharmed, but he was deeply saddened that he had lost his hound which protected his goods and his cattle from the many marauders in the neighborhood. Now all would be lost. When Culann expressed these regrets, the child replied: "No great matter. I will rear you a whelp from the same litter, and until it is grown and capable of action, I will be the hound that protects your cattle and yourself." "Cu Chulaind will be your name henceforth," Cathub happily replied. "I prefer my own name," said Setantae.

Cu Chulaind

Setantae was Deichtine's young son,
　　Whose name all ascertained.
But he'd soon lose this lovely name,
　　And be called Cu Chulaind.

The reason for this monstrous change,
　　Occurred at Culann's feast.
When this young lad arrived quite late
　　He had to kill a beast.

The hound of Culann was on guard
　　Of all that he possessed.
It was a very vicious dog,
　　When it was fetterless.

It took nine men to hold him firm,
　　With three chains wrapped about him.
So when Setantae neared the beast,
　　All thought they'd be without him.

But this young boy with his bare hands
　　Destroyed the vicious hound.
Then Culann's heavy heart was filled
　　With sadness quite profound.

This dog had long protected him
　　And everything he owned,
Now he, his cattle, and his flocks,
　　To thieves would be most prone.

He somehow felt that all was lost,
　　Until Setantae spoke.
He volunteered to play watchdog,
　　In place of what he choked.

The household now was much relieved,
　　For it would still be guarded.
They sang the praises of this lad,
　　So brave and lion-hearted.

Then Cathub changed Setantae's name,
　　And called him Cu Chulaind,
The hound that guards what Culann owns,
　　And watchfulness maintained.

Setantae wished to keep his name,
　　And be not called a dog.
But somehow nicknames always stick,
　　To join names' catalogue.

Thus Irish are called Mick or Mac,
　　Such nicknames we've all heard.
I'd rather hear these virile names,
　　Than Ogden Smith the Third.

Thus if your kids are Irish kids,
　　You know their future traits.
So give them names that fit them well,
　　Lest nickname compensates.

Fun with Irish Myths

You know your kids will like their fun,
    And probably like to fight.
They'll have a million-dollar smile,
    And eyes that sparkle bright.

Their wits will be both sharp and quick,
    That stories fabricate.
It's not that they are liars,
    They just exaggerate.

They'll always be where action is,
    And probably be its cause.
They'll be well-liked by other kids,
    And win their quick applause.

They'll really be quite genuine
    And obviously good.
They'll be in lots of trouble, though,
    And be misunderstood.

These are some things to think about,
    When picking out their names.
Let names bespeak their heritage,
    Which Celtic pride acclaims.

So give them names that match their worth,
    Like Kevin, Pat, or Mike.
Not silly little cutsie names,
    That only poodles like.

Some Early Adventures of Cu Chulaind

One day while Cathub was teaching druidry to one hundred pupils, Cu Chulaind was listening. A pupil asked his teacher what that particular day would be good for. Cathub answered that any warrior who took up arms that day would be famous among the men of Eriu and tales of his fame would be told forever. When Cu Chulaind heard this, he rushed to Conchubur and asked for arms. He smashed all the weapons that were given him as totally inferior until Conchubur gave him his own royal weapons to use.

Cathub expressed concern to Conchubur that he would give weapons to one so young. Conchubur then asked Cathub why he himself had suggested it. When Cathub told him that he had never made such a suggestion, the king called for the child and asked why he had lied. The youth told his uncle that he had overheard Cathub explain to his pupils that morning that fame awaited those who took up arms that day. And Cu Chulaind added: "If I am famous, I will be happy to live just one day."

The next day Cu Chulaind again listened to the lessons of Cathub. Again a pupil asked what that day would be good for. Cathub replied: "Anyone who steps into a chariot today will be known to the Eriu forever." Again Cu Chulaind went to Conchubur and sought and received a chariot as well as Ibor, Conchubur's own charioteer. The lad told Ibor to drive as far as the road leads. On the road they met Conall Cernach, a warrior whose turn it was to guard the province that day. Cu Chulaind told the warrior to return to his fort, for he would stand guard in his place that day.

As they drove about, Ibor explained the land and mountains and forts to the young boy. He pointed out the fort of the three sons of Nechta Scene, Foill, Fannall, and Tuachell, the great enemies of the Ulaid. These three claimed that there were not more men of Ulaid alive than they had slain. Cu Chulaind insisted that Ibor drive him to the fort in spite of the danger that Ibor insisted would be present. "Not to avoid danger have we come," said Cu Chulaind.

The sons of Nechta Scene saw Cu Chulaind coming and set out to meet him. When they arrived, Ibor sought to appease them by pointing out that here was just a little boy who was making an excursion in his chariot. Ibor was told to take the boy from the land. Cu Chulaind then bravely challenged Foill to combat. He thrust his spear at the angry Foill, broke his back, and took his head as well as his weapons. He next slew Fannall, and he finally slew Tuachell, the last of the three brothers. Taking their heads and their weapons he set out for Emuin Machae. The enemy set out in pursuit, but Ibor drove the horses so fast that they overtook the winds.

Coming upon a herd of deer Cu Chulaind asked Ibor if the Ulaid would think it better to bring a deer back dead or alive. Anyone can bring one back dead, he was told, but not alive. So Cu Chulaind seized a deer, tamed it and tied it to the chariot.

He then saw a flock of swans and asking the same question he received the same answer. He hurled a stone and dropped eight of the swans. The boy threw another stone and dropped twelve more. The swans were tied to the chariot also. He arrived back at Emuin Machae with the three heads in his chariot, the swans flying overhead, and the deer following behind.

At this point Cu Chulaind was wild with the fury of the hero. He was almost on fire. The warriors of the Ulaid seized him and thrust him into a vat of cold water. The first vat broke immediately from the excessive heat of the fury. When he was placed in the second vat, the water sizzled from the heat and then formed enormous bubbles. The third vat finally cooled him down. Mugain, Conchubur's wife, placed a mantle over him and he fell asleep on Conchubur's knees. He was now a lad of seventeen. Adventures and great feats would be in store for him in the years to come. Eventually he would become Ireland's greatest hero.

Cu Chulaind on the Loose

Young Cu Chulaind when just a boy,
    Once heard a druid teaching.
"Whoever took up arms that day,
    His fame would be far reaching."

So Cu Chulaind asked Conchubur,
    And got the king's own weapons.
The youth then got a chariot,
    And then soon went a steppin'.

Brave Ibor was the charioteer
    Of Conchubur, the king.
He drove the youth throughout the land,
    while on his youthful fling.

They met Ulaid's great enemies,
    The sons of Nechta Scene.
Who bragged they killed more Ulaid men,
    Than now could still be seen.

Then Cu Chulaind beheaded each,
    And put the heads aboard.
He set out for Emuin Machae,
    To give them to his lord.

His fury now to frenzy rose,
    He was about to burn.
They placed him in a cold vat,
    To make him taciturn.

Today we wonder at our teens.
    We think that they are hopeless.
We'd surely like to help them out.
    We'd like to make them dopeless.

When kids were very little tykes
    We potty-trained the lot.
But now that they have grown so much,
    We want them off the pot.

Lest parents grow discouraged now,
    Just think of Cu Chulaind.
No teen today could act much worse,
    If even on cocaine.

He beat up on his enemies,
    And took their heads to boot.
So full of pride was this young man,
    His will was absolute.

He thought of no one but himself,
    This very selfish lad.
A victim of his times and age,
    More than if he were bad.

So do not judge too quickly youth,
    For they are great within.
They hide it from their parents though,
    Who can't translate their grin.

The Making of a Hero

The hero's personality was defined to some extent by the number of "excellences" (buada) he possessed, the number of feats he could accomplish (clessa), and the number of gessa with which he was burdened. These were the things that distinguished the hero from ordinary mortals.

Cu Chulaind had many excellences — in beauty, in judgment, in swimming, in horsemanship, in valor, in counsel, in fine language, and in taking plunder. The ardor of his fury could heat three vats of water. He could go without sleep from Samhain until the following harvest. The wounds which he inflicted on others, even upon the Morrigan, could be healed only by himself. The Morrigan were three evil goddesses who continually made war upon men. They were the goddesses of war and death and slaughter, named Babdbh, Nemhain, and Macha. These war goddesses did not engage in battle. Their weapons were the magic and the terror they inflicted by their presence.

There were many feats that Cu Chulaind alone could do — the salmon's leap, the wheel's turn, killing eight out of nine men with a single spear, and tricks of fakerism. But he lacked the one luxury which mythology readily attributed to heroes, the gift of invulnerability. After any fight every part of his body was wounded. His body was so battered that birds could fly between his ribs.

The hero's superiority was not confined only to warfare and magic, it extended also to culture. The hero was familiar with poetry, with kennings and riddles. The hero did have limits, however. These limits were called his "gessa," things that he was not allowed to do. If gessa were violated the hero was doomed to defeat, at least to the extent of the violation. The hero Cu Chulaind had many gessa. Eventually their violation would bring about his death.

All heroes were expected to marry to preserve order among other warriors and their wives. All the women of Ulster were charmed by a hero, especially by Cu Chulaind. The choice of a wife was left to each hero and Cu Chulaind chose Emer, daughter of Forgall Monach. Emer's father was opposed to the marriage, for ritual convention required that every marriage be a kind of abduction. Her father imposed a further condition: Cu Chulaind must learn warfare from the evil goddess, Queen Scathach.

Cu Chulaind set out with two companions to visit the realm of Scathach. The two companions in fear of those mysterious and frightening regions soon abandoned him. But the hero always persevered when others turned back. And so Cu Chulaind escorted by monsters and crossing abysses peopled by phantoms, arrived at the gates that guarded the kingdom of Scathach. The Queen granted him three wishes. She instructed him, gave him her daughter, and foretold his career. In return Cu Chulaind must conquer her sister, Queen Aife, who loved nothing except horses and chariots. Soon Aife was subdued by Cu Chulaind who obtained from her the promise of three wishes. She would be the vassal of Scathach, she would sleep with him, and she would bear him a son. Aife later bore Cu Chulaind a son, Conlai, who would be killed by his father in single combat.

Cu Chulaind then returned home to claim Emer for his wife. For a whole year he tried to enter her home but was prevented from doing so by guards who were comrades of her three brothers. He then abducted Emer by force and married her. He later had an affair with Fand, the wife of Manannan, the son of the sea god Ler. The women of Ulster, all friends of Emer, were intent upon killing Fand.

Manannan arrived in time to save her and took her back with him to his kingdom in the sea. Cu Chulaind grew angry and despondent until druids brought him a drink of forgetfulness. Manannan shook his cloak between Cu Chulaind and Fand that they might never meet again.

The Personal Life of a Hero

A hero had both charms and spells,
　　With which his life was blessed,
No wonder ladies fell for him,
　　They thought he was the best.

The heroe's marriage was prescribed,
　　So men could keep their wives.
For if the hero freely roamed,
　　The queens might leave their hives.

The wife he had he freely chose.
　　The choice was up to him.
And heroes, blessed with great insight,
　　Don't pick them by a whim.

The careful choice of Cu Chulaind
　　On pretty Emer fell.
She was most fair and beautiful,
　　And beauty cast its spell.

Her father placed conditions though,
　　Before the two could wed.
He had to learn the art of war
　　From Scathach whom all dread.

He traversed over barren lands
　　To where her kingdoms lie.
He learned from her the art of war
　　And then he bid goodbye.

Fun with Irish Myths

And still Emer was kept from him,
    Protected by her brother.
So Cu Chulaind broke in the house,
    For he would wed no other.

But when in time romance wears thin,
    A husband's eyes will roam.
He found another pretty thing,
    And took her to his home.

Fand was the wife of Manannan,
    The son of sea god Ler.
When Manannan rejected her,
    Our hero set his snare.

Emer was set aside for Fand,
    By love sick Cu Chulaind.
She then set forth in words most wise,
    The following refrain.

"The new is bright; the tall is fair.
    What's near is very stale.
The unknown's loved; the known's ignored.
    The truth is fairytale."

How wise these words that Emer spoke!
    What lessons they contain!
So meditate on each of them,
    And peace and joy will reign.

These warning words of Emer, then,
    Are really quite sublime.
The words she spoke to Cu Chulaind
    Speak to our present time.

Our world's impressed with novelty.
    The new is much revered.
We think it bright, but it's quite dull,
    And often insincere.

So don't exchange the tested good,
    For what just comes along.
You'll soon forget its foolishness,
    And find that you were wrong.

And what is near is thought quite stale,
    As we take it for granted.
It's 'cause the distant isn't clear,
    That by it we're enchanted.

We sometimes tire of what is close,
    And look to greener fields.
Forgetting that we loved it once,
    And treasured what it yields.

And why is it the unknown's loved?
    This simply cannot be.
To love and not to know someone
    Is contradictory.

Fun with Irish Myths

Such things produce but one night stands,
    Not love but an affair.
It's this that makes men chauvinists,
    Who think they're debonair.

And what we know to be so good,
    We seem to just ignore.
That which we often cast aside,
    Is what we should adore.

Nor is the truth just fairytale,
    Nor fantasy nor myth.
But when truth makes demands on us,
    We banish it forthwith.

Indignant friends struck out at Fand,
    Protesting her transgression.
Then Manannan returned to claim
    What had been his possession.

When Fand went off with Manannan,
    Cu Chulaind was depressed.
He went into the hills alone,
    And there he convalesced.

A drink the druids brought him there
    Induced forgetfulness,
When he returned to start anew,
    He was temptationless.

Then Manannan, the god of sea,
   Shook cloak between these two,
So they would never meet again
   In secret rendezvous.

Good morals do not make good myths,
   As modern "soaps" proclaim.
In which we find these tales retold,
   But by another name.

But they have lost their fantasy,
   And have become quite dull,
Insulting our intelligence,
   Which TV has annulled.

Turn off the tube; pick up a book,
   And read these ancient tales.
And you will find more sense from them,
   Than all dear Abigails.

These myths will challenge you to think,
   Which TV seldom can.
You'll grown through wisdom of the past,
   And be myths' greatest fan.

The Death of a Hero

The final mark of the hero was a violent death. The dilemma of every heroic story was to reconcile the hero's death with invincibility. His death must somehow flow from deception so that it be not seen as a weakness. Cu Chulaind's death resulted from the dilemma of contradictory gessa, things he must or may not do. If he defiles his gessa, he is defenseless in battle.

Cu Chulaind had nineteen gessa. He was forbidden to pass by a hearth without tasting its food and he was forbidden to taste the flesh of dogs. As he passed by a hearth on the night of his death, the children of Calatin who had planned his death were cooking a dog.

A hero's death was always foretold by a druid. Thus the hero went through life knowing precisely what his end would be. As Cu Chulaind rode to his final battle a number of things warned him of his approaching death. Thrice fifty maidens who loved him watched as he left, for they knew he would not return. He was victimized by his gessa and broke them all in the same night.

The sons of Calatin who had studied wizardry for seventeen years carefully planned the death of Cu Chulaind. They had been mutilated by him, losing their right foot and their left hand. As the hero entered battle on this given night, the sons of

Calatin had made a fence of linked shields. At each corner Erc, the son of Cairpre, had placed two of his best warriors pretending to fight each other. Cu Chulaind hurled his spear at them. But whenever he would hurl his spear, the enemy would pick it up and hurl it back. In this way Lugaid, son of Cu Roi, killed Loeg, the loyal charioteer of Cu Chulaind, and Erc killed the Grey of Macha, Cu Chulaind's steed. The third time that Cu Chulaind hurled his spear, Lugaid hurled it back and killed the hero of the Ulaid. Cu Chulaind's bowels came out and he went to the lake to wash. An otter (water dog) came to the lake and drank his blood. Cu Chulaind threw a stone at the otter and killed it. It had long been foretold that his last heroic deed would be like his first, the killing of a dog.

Lugaid then came forth to take his head. As Cu Chulaind died his sword fell and cut off the right hand of Lugaid. Lugaid then cut off Cu Chulaind's right hand as well as his head to seek revenge. In the circumstances surrounding the hero's death the storyteller actualizes the impossible. Myth is not bound by the laws of nature. It transcends the limitations of common sense. These were stories told by word of mouth, not stories written down. It was natural then that these stories would grow and become more complex with each telling, for they were told not just to teach, but to entertain.

The Tale of Macc Da Tho's Pig

A famous king was Macc Da Tho,
    And he possessed a hound.
This dog's fame spread throughout the land,
    For reasons that were sound.

The king and queen of Connacht land,
    King Ailill and Queen Medb,
Asked Macc Da Tho for gifted hound;
    They needed it they said.

Then messengers from Ulstermen
    Came with the same request.
The dog, Ailbe, was sought by them,
    And their need was no less.

So Macc Da Tho was much confused.
    He couldn't eat or sleep.
His wife told him to please both sides,
    And see what he could reap.

So hound was promised to each group,
    Not knowing what would be.
For problems of some future day,
    Were more than Macc could see.

Both parties came for promised hound,
    The same time and same day.
And all were asked to banquet hall,
    For pig that he would slay.

A large pig then was carried in
    With forty oxen on it.
The question rose, "Who'd carve the pig?"
    And both sides thought upon it.

Bricriu said: "Let combat be!"
    That's how we shall decide.
Ailill and Conchubur then said,
    That, too, would be their pride.

Then all began to brag and boast.
    Connachta's Cet took knife.
"If there be one more strong than I,
    Let that man take my life."

Some Ulaid stood to challenge Cet,
    Who put them in their place.
He told how he had conquered them,
    And they sat down disgraced.

Then Conall Cernach, Ulaid's Pride,
    Arrived for King Macc's feast.
And stated that he killed each day,
    One Connacht man at least.

He stated that he never slept,
    Less pillowed by a head,
He'd taken from Connachta men,
    That he had left for dead.

Fun with Irish Myths

Embarrassed Cet then quickly said,
    He knew who could defeat him.
It was a pity he wasn't there,
    This Anluan who'd beat him.

Then Conall reached into his bag.
    And pulled from it a head,
Anluan's head, which startled all,
    Its blood still running red.

Then grabbing knife he carved the pig,
    And ate the choicest parts.
He gave the Ulaid all the best,
    With which the fighting starts.

Then everyone hit someone else,
    And Ailbe was set loose.
He nipped at all Connachta men,
    A part of King Macc's ruse.

The charioteer of King Ailill,
    Hit Ailbe with a pole.
And where the hound's head once had been,
    There now was just a hole.

And so the Ulaid won the day,
    Connachta men were routed.
And poets would forever sing,
    The glory Cet had doubted.

So if you are invited to
    An Irish home for dinner.
Know that the one who carves the pig
    Is said to be the winner.

If you, by chance, are asked to carve
    The pig upon the table.
Just smile and take the knife and do
    The best that you are able.

But if another grabs that knife,
    And cuts it in your stead,
Don't make too great a fuss of it,
    Or you might lose your head.

Bricriu's Feast

The mischief maker, Bricriu,
    Was called the poison-tongued,
Like Loki of the Nordic Myths.
    But he was Irish-tongued.

He once invited Ulstermen
    To come to his grand feast.
A year was spent preparing it,
    Or near that time, at least.

The invitations were declined,
    Without too much misgiving.
For if they went, they knew their dead
    Would far exceed their living.

He threatened strife of every kind,
    If they would not attend.
And so they came, though unenthused,
    And were so 'til the end.

When they arrived Bricriu tried
    Inciting them to fight
About who was the champion
    And who'd be at king's right.

At first he tempted brave Loeguere,
    By flattering his skills.
The same he did to Conall, too.
    That's how he got his thrills.

And then he went to Cu Chulaind,
 And cunningly he said:
"All warriors that will challenge you,
 Will be without a head."

All Ulaid's warriors were on hand,
 And bards and entertainers.
Musicians played; buffoons performed,
 And there were no complainers.

When feast was set the host cried out,
 "Behold the champion measure.
May Ulaid's greatest warrior now
 Take it for his pleasure."

The servants of the bravest three,
 Called: "Bring it over here."
Then as the three of them stood up,
 Their spears and swords appeared.

Loeguere and Conall then set out,
 Pursuing Cu Chulaind.
Senchae then said to Conchubur:
 "What can such action gain?"

And so the king stepped in between,
 And all the fighting ceased.
For Senchae was the earthly god,
 Invited to this feast.

Fun with Irish Myths

"Next day we'll go to King Ailill,
    And ask of him the question.
And he will solve who's best of you."
    This was Senchae's suggestion.

Then Bricriu still pondered how
    He'd get the wives to fight,
To make great fools of themselves,
    As husbands did that night.

He talked to all the warriors' wives,
    About who'd enter first.
He promised she'd be belle of ball.
    All others would be cursed.

So warriors' wives with all their maids
    Made beeline for the door.
And all within and all without,
    Took part in their uproar.

Then Senchae once again spoke up
    To criticize their actions.
He closed the door to each of them,
    So there would be no factions.

"An evil night," said Conchubur,
    "Your actions are absurd.
A war with weapons we'll not have.
    We'll have a war with words."

Each woman then drew back from door,
    Protected by her mate.
While each began to praise her spouse,
    The others she'd berate.

Each spouse performed as he was praised,
    Nor was he in a hurry.
They shook the house with feats performed
    In their heroic fury.

When morning came the warriors left,
    And set out for the king,
Who'd judge who was the best of them,
    To stop their bickering.

And as they rode through countryside,
    They came upon a fog.
They had to stop until it passed,
    Or fall into a bog.

Each met a giant when he stopped,
    And by him was restrained.
Loeguere and Conall fled from him,
    But not so Cu Chulaind.

The giant fled from Cu Chulaind,
    Not Cu Chulaind from giant.
There was no doubt about the best,
    But Conall was defiant.

Fun with Irish Myths

"The giant must have been a friend,"
    Said Conall and Loeguere.
"That's why he favored Cu Chulaind,
    And that's not really fair."

They then set out for Ailills' fort,
    The warriors and the king,
Their servants and their ladies loved,
    And all that they could bring.

Ailill said that he'd need three days
    To judge the matter rightly.
And so all left except the three
    Whom everyone thought knightly.

That evening three druidic beasts
    Were set free from their cave.
Loeguere and Conall fled from them.
    The third was much more brave.

Cu Chulaind struck a blow to beasts.
    The beasts then settled down.
All night the hero stood his guard,
    Which surely won renown.

Loeguere and Conall disagreed.
    Cu Chulaind didn't win.
It is not beasts that heroes fight.
    What they must fight are men.

The many other tests they took
    Proved Cu Chulaind the best.
Loeguere and Conall spurned them all,
    As not the best of tests.

Then finally someone came forth,
    Who'd be a worthy judge.
Uath, who could transform his shape
    With his druidic nudge.

They all agreed to let him judge.
    They would accept his word.
I think they all had second thoughts,
    About what each one heard.

He told them they must take the axe,
    And then cut off his head.
And when tomorrow came along,
    He'd cut off theirs instead.

In turn, all three cut off his head,
    The first part of the plan.
But when there came the second part,
    The two were not on hand.

But when it came to Cu Chulaind,
    He stretched his neck on block.
Then three times Uath swung his axe,
    But each time it would lock.

Fun with Irish Myths

Uath pronounced that Cu Chulaind
    Was champion of Erin.
Again the others disagreed,
    And said his word was barren.

The final test of warriorship
    Was at Cu Rui's fort.
The king was absent at the time,
    But had in mind great sport.

The three were asked to guard the fort
    On alternating nights.
A giant came and battled them.
    The first two fled in fright.

But Cu Chulaind defeated him.
    Who then exchanged for life,
Supremacy for Cu Chulaind,
    Precedence for his wife.

So if you have an argument,
    About the best of peers.
Just use this test from Irish myths,
    And watch them disappear.

But just be sure that in the test,
    The other's head first dances.
For if it is the other way,
    You boldly blew your chances.

The Origins of Gaelic

Before the Tower of Babel
    There was a single tongue.
And it was spoken everywhere,
    By both the old and young.

That language was called Gorthigern.
    Which now is known as Hebrew.
One time it was the only tongue,
    That any man alive knew.

Soon after Nimrod's ego trip,
    And tower had been built.
Man's conversations grew confused,
    His speech looked like a quilt.

Here's how these strange things did occur,
    How Gaelic came to be.
Before men knew of Ireland
    Out in the western sea.

Nimrod was Tzar of all that was.
    He longed to build a tower.
He called his seventy-two chiefs,
    Who came within the hour.

While they were laying bricks and stones,
    Their tongues became confused.
And no one even understood
    The words that others used.

Fun with Irish Myths

So seventy-two languages
    Then suddenly appeared,
Each one quite different from the rest,
    Some funny and some weird.

From that day on Chief Fenius spoke
    A language that was new.
He gave it to his family
    So they would speak it too.

Nel was the son of Fenius,
    Nel's son was Gaedil Glas.
From Gaedil Gaelic took its name,
    A name with lots of class.

This language is not spoken much.
    Today it's not in vogue.
But Irish speaking any tongue,
    Will butcher it by brogue.

Their brogue is hard to understand,
    Unless you read their eyes,
That sparkle full of meaning and
    So often hypnotize.

They speak with wit and friendliness,
    And laugh between each word.
They're never at a loss to speak,
    But they are seldom heard.

Why Ireland Has No Snakes

There never was a serpent or
    A monster of the world
That made its den in Ireland,
    Or there its tail unfurled.

There are no snakes in Ireland,
    Nor were they ever there.
To credit this to Patrick,
    To Moses isn't fair.

The reason for their absence is
    A promise Moses made,
When asked by Gaedil's father, Nel
    To come to Gaedil's aid.

Nel lived in Egypt in those days,
    And Moses lived there too.
Nel was forefather of the Celts,
    While Moses was a Jew.

A snake had bitten Nel's young son.
    He was about to die.
Nel called on holy Moses then
    To offer prayers on high.

The son got well and Moses gave
    A blessing on the spot.
The prophet promised Gaedil then,
    Where he lived, snakes would not.

Fun with Irish Myths

Yes, any land where Gaedil lived
    Would always be snake-free.
So when he went to Ireland,
    No serpent could he see.

That probably was the first time,
    I'm sure it was the last,
That Irish cured their snake bites
    With prayer instead of glass.

Does every Irishman then have
    Mixed feelings for a snake?
Must he be bitten on his foot
    To eat and have his cake?

No, there's preventive medicine,
    Developed best by Celts.
So just in case some snake should bite,
    They take their daily belts.

Another blessing Moses gave
    That brings the Irish joy
Was kings and lords and saints would be
    Descended from this boy.

That's why the Irish are so proud
    To be just what they are,
More so than any other race,
    More so, I'd say, by far.

Yes, they are proud of Ireland,
    The land on which they trod,
For there they are, as Moses said,
    A people blessed by God.

The Irish Blessing

The Irishman is famous for
    His blessing or his curse.
So things could get much better soon,
    Or things could get much worse.

These Irishmen like elephants
    Are quite slow to forget.
If one becomes your enemy,
    You'll know and you'll regret.

But if you have one for a friend,
    Great loyalty you'll see.
For faithfulness has always been
    The Irish guarantee.

His curse will bring out hidden hates
    Found in the ancient Celt,
Who lopped off heads and burned at stakes
    And other tortures dealt.

But blessings bring out all the faith
    For which most Celts are known,
Which first begins in works of love
    And then becomes full blown.

A Celt who's not a man of faith,
    Turns to iconoclast.
He soon becomes barbarian
    As he relives his past.

Fun with Irish Myths

He'll put aside all sacred things,
　　Forgetting how to think.
He'll boast about himself a lot,
　　And give himself to drink.

Without a faith he soon reverts
　　To all his pagan past,
A cruel, brutal form of life,
　　Sown by druidic caste.

So build your life upon a faith.
　　Bring out the best within you.
Don't pick and choose just what you like,
　　For faith can't be a menu.

Recall the blessing Moses gave
　　To Nel the intercedent,
Nel, the son of Fenius,
　　Our Celtic antecedent.

So seek the blessings Irish give,
　　And happiness you'll know.
As God and angels shower you
　　With graces as you go.

The Finian Cycle

The Finian cycle in Irish mythology deals with a group of stories about the Fianna Erinn, a group of men under the leadership of Finn Mac Cumbal during the reign of Cormac Mac Art. Cormac was an Irish king of the third century, celebrated by bards for his wisdom and his hospitality. He organized the Fianna to secure governments, order, and peace. "The world was full of goodness in the time of Cormac. There was peace and ease and happiness in his time."

The Fianna was a band of roving men who engaged continuously in war or hunting. There were three regiments each with three thousand men. In times of war it was larger. The Fianna was formed to defend any Irish prince assailed by a foreign foe. It guarded the coasts of Ireland. The members of the Fianna supported themselves by hunting and fishing.

There were four gessa laid on each member of the Fianna. (1) He must never seek a dowry with his wife, but choose her for her goodness and virtue. (2) He must never offer violence to a woman. (3) He must never refuse hospitality. (4) He must never turn his back on adversity in battle. The physical requirements demanded of those who would enter the Fianna were severe. They would have to jump over a branch as high as their head and stoop under one as low as their knee while running at full speed. They never used horses for they ran as fast. Others may be stronger than the men of the Fianna, but none was more wise, none more gentle to women nor more generous to men, nor was any man more true to his word than the member of the Fianna.

Finn was the son of Cumhal, leader of the Clann Biscayne. Cumhal was slain by the Clann Morna, commanded by Goll Mac Morna. Cumhal's wife bore a posthumous son. He was raised secretly to conceal him from the Clann Morna. He was fair-haired and excelled in all sports. "Who was this fair-haired boy?" all asked who saw him. That is why he was called Finn.

On one occasion he cooked the salmon of wisdom for an old man. He scalded his thumb and sucked it to ease the pain. By accident, then, he tasted the salmon of wisdom. After that he had only to suck his thumb to receive knowledge. When he grew up he was chosen to lead his father's old clan. He united it with the Clann Morna. The two came to be called the "Fianna Eirinn." Finn's home was in the hills of Kildare.

Finn had two sons, Fergus and Oisin. Fergus was the envoy of the Fianna; Oisin was its bard. The one-eyed Goll was the enemy of Finn's father, but he was loyal to Finn. The finest character of the Fianna was Diarmait. He was brave, untarnished in honor, generous, and never boastful.

After Finn's wife died he was quite restless and his servant suggested that he marry Grania, the daughter of Cormac, the king of Ireland. When this marriage was proposed to Grania by her father, she replied: "If he be a fitting son-in-law to you, why shouldn't he be a fitting husband to me?" The marriage was then arranged between Finn and Grania. The Fianna travelled to Tara where Cormac was to place the hand of his daughter into the hand of Finn. At the feast Grania told the druid Mac Morna that it would be better for her to marry Oisin, the son of Finn, for he was more her age. There were also others there that she would rather marry, Goll, Caelte, Mac Lugaid, Diarmait, and others.

Grania then sent her handmaid with a drink for Finn and drugged it with a cunning drug. Finn fell into a stupor. Cormac drank of it as did his wife Eitche. All fell asleep. Grania then went to Diarmait and said: "Will you receive courtship from me?" He replied, "No." He could not hurt his chief. She then obliged him by the gessa that he must always come to the aid of a woman in need. Oisin advised him to go with her but to watch out for the wiles of Finn. Caelte advised the same. Diarmait then shook hands with the chieftains that he would never see again and left with Grania.

At daybreak the sleepers awoke and discovered what had happened, that Grania and Diarmait had stolen away. Finn summoned his trackers and told them to find Diarmait and Grania. Each time the trackers got near, Oisin and the other friends of Diarmait warned him that Finn was close. One day while he was hiding in the woods after many months of flight, from the ever-pursuing Finn, the boar of Gulban attacked Diarmait and mortally wounded him. Finn by his magical powers could have healed the wounded warrior with a draught of water, but he refused. After that the Fianna never revered their chieftain again.

Finn later married Grania. The Fianna's power had greatly declined. There were many dissensions between the clans, and Finn was later killed by rebellious members of the Fianna at the Ford of Brea on the Boyne. His grandson Oscar, the son of Oisin, became the leader.

After Cormac's death, the members of the Fianna quarreled with King Cairbre who succeeded Cormac. War broke out and Oscar was killed by Cairbre. Almost all the Finians were killed in the battle. King Cairbre died later from wounds received in that battle. Only Caelte and Oisin survived. Caelte went to live among the Tuatha De Danann and Oisin married Niamh, the daughter of a sea god and went with her to the Land of the Young where he stayed for three hundred years.

After those many years he longed to see Ireland again and decided to go there. Niamh made him promise not to set a foot on Irish soil. When he arrived on the fairy steed, he inquired about the Fianna. It no longer existed. Everything had changed.

Men had grown weak. He saw three hundred men trying to lift a marble slab. He rode to assist them. As he did so, he accidentally slipped from his magical horse and his foot touched the earth. Instantly the fairy steed vanished. Oisin rose from the earth no longer a strong young man, but an old man, blind and grey and withered.

These and other tales make up the Finian cycle in Irish mythology. The Finian cycle is less heroic in its deeds than the Ulster cycle and less magical than the Mythological cycle. But it is more romantic than both.

The Fianna

A band of warriors all most brave,
    Led by their chieftain Finn,
Protected all of Ireland,
    Lest foes would do it in.

All were athletic, robust men
    To whom king had recourse.
They could perform most daring feats,
    And then outrun a horse.

One Finn Mac Cumhal organized
    These men into a clan,
To aid the kings of Ireland
    And offer them their hand.

He was a man both good and wise.
    No wiser man was known.
The wisdom of the salmon cooked,
    This Finn had made his own.

He cooked it for another man,
    And scalded his right thumb.
To ease the pain he sucked on it,
    Then wise he did become.

Druidic wisdom came with taste
    Of Irish salmon cooked.
The only difficulty was
    To get the darned thing hooked.

He didn't show much wisdom though
 In picking out a wife.
He chose one only half his age,
 And this caused future strife.

Although she said she'd marry him,
 Grania changed her mind.
She set her eyes on younger men,
 And they weren't hard to find.

When Finn then came a courting her,
 She drugged the old guy's drinks.
She then eloped with Diarmait,
 While Finn caught forty winks.

When Finn woke up and found this out,
 He boiled, to say the least.
He gathered troops and said to them:
 "Let suitor be deceased!"

The chase went on for many months,
 The subject of this tale.
But in the end the suitor fell,
 By Gulban's boar impaled.

Old Finn could heal with magic charms,
 But he refused to do so.
Dairmait died while Finn looked on
 As Grania lost her trousseau.

Fun with Irish Myths

Finn married her but lost the hold
    He had upon his men.
For callousness and ruthlessness
    All decencies offend.

And when Finn died by traitor's hand,
    The Fian fell apart.
From peak so high he tumbled far,
    This Irish Bonaparte.

This myth just read could teach us much,
    As past things we relive.
For things once thought ridiculous
    Today a lesson give.

Some kid in seeking to be wise,
    Like Finn, might suck his thumb.
His parents are embarrassed then,
    And think the kid is dumb.

Or if they see a salmon that
    Is hanging from his teeth,
They only see the foolishness,
    And not the brains beneath.

Oisin

Young Oisin was the son of Finn,
    And he survived Finn's fall.
He married Niamh of the sea,
    Who heard her lover's call.

They settled in the Land of Young,
    Where aging is unknown.
And even after centuries,
    No one has ever grown.

But when three hundred years had passed,
    Oisin missed Erin shores.
He longed to pay a visit there,
    And open its closed doors.

Niamh gave him her fairy steed
    With orders very clear.
"Don't set a foot upon the soil,
    Not even for a beer!"

Oisin rode out for Ireland,
    That island in the sea.
He soon discovered that all things,
    Weren't what they used to be.

Men were not strong as they once were,
    Nor were they brave or wise.
They weren't as tall as they had been.
    Most now were just pint sized.

Fun with Irish Myths

He saw weak men who couldn't lift
    Some marble off the ground,
Just one of many baffling things
    In Ireland he found.

He stopped his horse to help these men,
    But slipped and touched the earth.
Then all the blessings he had had,
    Quite promptly lost their worth.

The horse he rode just disappeared.
    No longer was he young,
A blind and grey and withered man,
    That quickly came unsprung.

The trouble with young Oisin was
    He catered to the crowds,
As he who was so far above,
    Descended from the clouds.

We sometimes think we serve men best,
    When we bend down to them,
Instead of lifting them to heights,
    Where they might find a gem.

We fool ourselves, but only selves.
    No other is deceived.
In hoping to fool other men,
    Our hope is misconceived.

So if you ever come to find
    The fountain that gives youth.
Don't let your curiosity
    Exchange it by a goof.

And if you ride a fairy steed,
    Don't touch your foot to ground,
But ride with head above the clouds
    Lest you come tumbling down.

The world we live in everyday
    Is not what it should be.
And if we anchor both feet there,
    We've lost our Odyssey.

So rise above the things of earth
    And find what Irish found.
You'll find it in their lovely myths,
    Where mysteries abound.

Go back in time and listen to
    The ancient Irish wisdom.
The Irish will proclaim to you,
    There is a better kingdom!

Just look at what the Irish were
    And what they have become.
And you will know what you can be
    If you're adventuresome.

Fun with Irish Myths

The wisdom of the druid's mind,
  The cry of the Banshee,
The chatter of the fairy-fold
  And of the people-wee.

These are the things that formed the past
  In Irish history.
They'll also cause when read today,
  A present ecstasy.

Don't be enslaved by what you are,
  But let yourself run free.
If Irish wisdom guides your step.
  Who knows what you can be.

We often fear to take that step,
  So never do arrive.
It's fear that keeps us where we are
  Just trying to survive.

But this is true in everything
  That we attempt to do.
Unless we first begin it,
  We never will get through.

Poets

The Ollam was the master bard,
　　Atop the heap of poets,
Who handed down their ancient past
　　So younger Celts would know it.

Their stories all were memorized.
　　There was no written word.
The only truths that Celtics knew
　　Were those that they had heard.

Apprenticeship for twenty years,
　　And trained in special schools.
They eulogized past history,
　　And praised the kings who ruled.

They loved alliteration's way
　　Of setting forth their rhymes.
An Irish characteristic,
　　Yet, even in our times.

They handed down their ancient thoughts
　　That we still have today.
We only know our treasured past
　　By what they had to say.

Celtic Immortality

The ancient Celts believed in life after death. Archaeology attests to this belief time and time again as it sets before us the contents and furnishings of Celtic graves. Lucan speaks of the druidic teaching that after death the souls of men continue to control their bodies in another world.

Celts accepted death without fear or sadness. It was only a juncture in a long life. Some would argue that at times Celts even preferred death to life. The Celtic otherworld was not the silent realm of Erebus or the gloomy place that Hades was in Greek mythology. It was more like the Elysian Fields where Greek heroes found rightful rewards.

The otherworld was a land of happiness and blessed living. Sickness and decay were totally unknown. Here one could find the pleasures of love without guilt. It was a land of beautiful women. It was filled with enchanting music from bright plumaged birds and from the swaying branches of otherworld trees. Here wonderful instruments sounded without being played. Here one could find an abundance of delicious food and pleasing drink from magical vessels of inexhaustible plenty. Here one could find whatever one sought. It was truly a land of every Celtic delight.

This land of eternal living was located far west of Ireland on three fifty islands. It was a colorful land of exciting beauty. There was no weeping or wailing. Treachery was unknown. There was never a harsh sound.

"There there is neither mine nor thine. White are teeth there, dark the brows. A delight of the eye the array of our hosts. Every cheek there is the hue of love. Purple the surface of every plain. Fine though you think the ale of Ireland, more exhilarating still the ale of Tir Mar. A wondrous land is the land I tell of. Youth does not give way to age there. Sweet warm streams flow through the land. The choice of meat and of wine. Splendid people without blemish. Conception without sin, without lust."

Labraid was the deity ruler of the otherworld. Mortals were led to this kingdom by otherworld people who guided them there. Often times Celtic mythology depicted death as more alluring than life.

Celtic After-Life

Yes, every man must have a faith,
    Or he must face despair.
If he denies causality,
    His head is filled with air.

Since order needs an orderer.
    Dame chance cannot be first.
Chance simply has no meaning then,
    Except as order's curse.

Chance presupposes harmony,
    For it is its exception.
And only if it's viewed that way,
    Can we glean its perception.

The Celts were smart enough to know
    That such things had to be.
They quickly recognized this fact,
    And didn't disagree.

The pagan Celts then believed in God,
    And held life after death.
They knew they'd have a place to go,
    When breathing final breath.

How sad that life without a goal!
    It must beget despair,
So haunted by approaching death,
    Which must seem quite unfair.

Fun with Irish Myths

Perhaps that's why all Irishmen
    Are full of life and fun.
They know a life will follow
    When life on earth is done.

The present they don't emphasize,
    Nor grief accentuate.
When living for tomorrow's joys,
    Things will eventuate.

One might think they are frivolous,
    But such is not the case.
They really are quite serious,
    And put all things in place.

So life and love and food and drink
    Are thoroughly enjoyed.
Though Irish believe in heaven's goal,
    They are not paranoid.

They know what life is all about,
    And live without a whimper.
That's why they're fun to be around,
    In spite of their quick temper.

They are a race of optimists.
    I'm sure you will agree.
They live on hope and confidence,
    The Irish pedigree.

Brigit

Some think of Brigit as a saint.
    If truth be known, she really "ain't."
She was a goddess Celts adored,
    And Irish wives at birth implored.

St. Brigit then usurped her role,
    And she's the saint we now extol.
She also took the goddess feast,
    Then goddess worship quickly ceased.

Forsaking chance to be a wife,
    She founded a religious life.
Then goddess Brigit disappeared,
    As Irish hearts the saint endeared.

The name means "the exalted one."
    And for the saint a name hard won.
She was a nun when nuns were nuns
    Before their lives became undone.

She knew St. Patrick in his day
    And for his work she daily prayed.
The patroness of Irish schools,
    Her charity rewrote their rules.

This saint the Irish still acclaim,
    As Irish kids receive her name.
That name sounds like an Irish smile.
    And what on earth is more worthwhile.

Some Thoughts on the Irish

The classic authors thought the Celts
    A lyric genius breed,
Susceptible to pouting fits,
    But eloquent, indeed.

Most prodigal in daily life,
    So volatile in make-up,
And brave beyond all common sense,
    Contentious when they wake up.

Ebullient in character,
    With personality.
But they are praised above all else,
    For hospitality.

So if you want some Irishman
    To list among your friends,
Put up with all his little faults,
    And win great dividends.

The price you pay is rather small,
    For what you will receive.
He'll bring you joy as well as fun,
    Though sometimes you might grieve.

So many contradictions then
    Are found within this race.
Just when you think you know them well,
    They don another face.

The Stubborn Irish

The Irish had a special love
    For lands on which they lived.
So brooks and mountain tops had names
    In Irish narrative.

They loved the land and sea and sky
    And everything around them.
But they disliked those many things,
    Which Irish felt had bound them.

They first disliked authority
    And centralized control.
There was a kind of anarchy
    Within the Celtic soul.

They were an independent lot.
    Each tribe was judged supreme.
Anarchy was their goal pursued,
    Authority, blasphemed.

And what was true in bygone days
    Is surely true today.
One thing the Irish surely know
    Is how to disobey.

An Irish Anomaly

Cheapskates are scorned by Irishmen.
    Among them they are rare.
But once you meet the Irish kind,
    No other can compare.

They're not just tight like Scotchmen are.
    They simply are just cheap.
They'll take advantage till they have,
    And what they have they'll keep.

And you cannot embarrass them
    To change their stingy soul.
For Irishmen not generous,
    Have lost all self-control.

Their cheapness is embarrassing,
    A family disgrace,
A puzzle to true Irishmen,
    A blight upon their race.

One wonders how they got so tight
    To sponge upon their friends,
For they are mostly wealthy men,
    Who clip their dividends.

Fun with Irish Myths

I'm sure they do not realize
    How very cheap they are.
They've practiced it so very long,
    Each has become a star.

They think no more of five cents than
    They do of their right arm.
They'd no more part with ten cents than
    Concede the family farm.

They probably think they're generous,
    Deceiving selves alone.
But Irish hold them in disgust.
    Skinflints they won't condone.

I'm sure you've met their type before,
    More often than you think.
You'll find them eating others' food,
    And drinking others' drink.

At any Irish gathering,
    They only bring themselves.
It never would occur to them,
    To put food on the shelves.

But don't let them arouse your wrath
    Or animosity.
They'll never know the Irish joy
    Of generosity.

Royal Elections are a Lot of Bull

The Irish had a funny way
    In which to choose their kings.
So is it any wonder, then,
    They had such ding-a-lings.

The king was chosen by a man,
    Who first devoured a bull,
He drank the blood that it had drained,
    Until he was quite full.

And then the man who ate the bull
    And all its blood consumed,
Laid down quite full and fell asleep,
    To dream, it was presumed.

When he awoke he named the king,
    The name, his dream's suggestion.
I think we could allude to this,
    As king by indigestion.

Perhaps that was a better plan
    Than what we have today,
Where dullards win high offices,
    And there they often stay.

I'd like to try that Celtic way,
    Though something might be missin'.
They only had to eat the bull,
    But to it we must listen.

Irish Night Mahrs

The world where elves and goblins live
    Exchanges night and day.
The night is day and day is night,
    All time has gone astray.

As demons walk the earth at night,
    Let Irishmen beware.
Especially of that evil one,
    They gave the name of "Mahr."

This female demon that they feared
    Slept on their chest at night.
And when she woke the Irish up,
    This night Mahr caused much fright.

So all night long these spirits roamed.
    But day put out their spark.
The crowing cock sent spirits home.
    As dawn dispelled the dark.

I know a lot of Irishmen
    Who still roam every night.
They have a drink at every bar
    To quench their appetite.

And like the goblins of the past
    They hear the crowing cock.
And then they stumble home to bed,
    As wife points to the clock.

Irish Heads Held High

The Irish had a thing for heads,
  And lopped them off with ease.
They kept them in a bag until,
  They hung them from their trees.

A victory was not complete,
  Until a head was taken.
The head was placed within a bag;
  The body was forsaken.

Each head became the boasting piece
  That they so oft displayed.
When bragging at the Celtic feast,
  Each head brought accolades.

It was a way of rousing fear,
  Among their enemy.
Thus heads were hung on chariot poles
  For every man to see.

They were displayed most visibly,
  That each foe might surmise,
If he would stick around to fight,
  His head might be the prize.

There's lots of modern Irishmen,
  I think have lost their heads.
When temper outruns reasoning,
  They act like quadrupeds.

The Irish Queen of Hearts

Medb was the queen of Connachtown,
 The wife of King Ailill.
But after she had married him,
 Her morals went down hill.

A queen's bad morals make good myths.
 And Medb was quite a lover.
Another man was waiting in
 The footprints of the other.

But when she first looked for a mate,
 How high her sights were set.
And if Medb did not compromise,
 She'd still be looking yet.

She ruled her realm from Cruachan,
 Where all men sought her hand.
But she declined each one of them,
 So great was her demand.

She asked a harder wedding gift
 Than any man could give.
No woman in all Ireland,
 Could be more lucrative.

The man who wished to marry her,
 Would pay a price most dear.
"No meanness could there be in him,
 No jealousy nor fear."

Euhemerisms

Euhemerisms treated gods
    As if they were but men,
Confusing faith and history,
    Without much discipline.

The monks made gods heroic men,
    So pagan cults would cease.
And scholars seemed to go along,
    All dupes of this caprice.

But all in all the Irish monks
    Were faithful to their task.
They handed on the Irish myths.
    And that's what history asked.

The Irish heroes we discussed
    Were worshipped once as gods.
Now each is just a creature who,
    Through history pages trods.

These myths were not just accidents,
    Nor facts of history,
But products of the Celtic soul,
    Instilling mystery.

That longed for Celtic freedom, then,
    That need of Celtic mind,
Was always just an Irish dream
    That history left behind.

Mananann

The most poetic god of all
    Was sea god Mananann.
He was the happy son of Ler,
    Named for the Isle of Man.

Wherever Mananann would roam,
    Within the Irish Sea,
The sea was sown with purple blooms,
    And salmons leaped with glee.

When goddesses would move about,
    He pulled their water cart.
He could assume most any form;
    For him it was an art.

This Mananann was Lord of Seas;
    Wild waves were but his studs.
The ruler of the otherworld,
    Who sometimes causes floods.

He now lives on charmed Arran's Isle,
    Along the Firth of Clyde,
Where he is ruler of the sid,
    And dwells near the seaside.

It's here he might be seen today,
    This ruler of the sea,
Still frolicking among the waves
    With purple garnishee.

The God of Light

Mac Cecht was just a human name,
    For Dian Cecht, the Sun,
Who travelled over Ireland,
    Before each day was done.

The Sun had many other names.
    But really all were one.
Mac Grene, Mac Cuill or Mac Cecht,
    Were all names for the Sun.

For Irish numbers emphasized,
    Great strength, not quantity.
And so they used the triple form.
    All gods were named in three.

The God of Darkness

Donn is the brown or darkness god,
    The Irish god of dead.
He bids all people come to him,
    When they lay on death's bed.

He is benign, yet terrible,
    Most contradictory.
He stands alone. He is aloof
    In Irish history.

The Ulster Curse

Fair Macha of the spirit world
    Married a mortal man,
A widower from Crunnchu town
    Of the Ulster clan.

This supernatural bride of his
    Could run much like a deer,
But he must never mention this,
    Lest others overhear.

She told him he must never speak
    About her to another,
Especially at this time when she's
    About to be a mother.

But any bragging Irishman
    Cannot be kept closed mouth,
And so the farmer quickly spoke
    About his speedy spouse.

At Ulster's great Assembly Race
    He spoke of his wife's speed.
That could outrace the king's great horse,
    And beat his finest steed.

The king then called the farmer's bluff,
    Demanding his wife run.
And then unless she'd beat his horse,
    The farmer's life was done.

The pregnant wife was forced to race
    Since king was rather cruel.
She should have been more prudent than
    To marry such a fool.

She beat the horse and won the race,
    Much to the king's chagrin.
But as she crossed the finish line,
    She gave birth there to twins.

In giving life she brought on death,
    While giving birth she died.
But with her dying breath she cursed
    The Ulstermen's great pride.

In times of peril or of need
    All Ulstermen would feel,
The pains and pangs of giving birth.
    This curse she'd not repeal.

They would be weak as she was weak,
    And ache as she now ached.
And robbed of strength before their foe,
    All victories they'd forsake.

Fun with Irish Myths

And when Queen Medb discovered this,
    Great Ulster she attacked.
But Cu Chulaind defended it,
    While men laid on their back.

Don't think you can outsmart your wife.
    She'll beat you every time.
Don't think you can just flatter her,
    Your words aren't worth a dime.

So watch your tongue and guard your speech,
    When challenging a dame.
For if she puts a curse on you,
    You'll never be the same.

Leprechauns

Wee people have their leprechauns,
    Shoemakers of the sid,
A greedy bunch of thieves are they
    'Neath Irish pyramid.

So never trust a leprechaun,
    If he repairs your shoe.
They're listed as most irritable,
    In meanness' Who's Who.

They're always causing problems that
    Most peaceful men can't solve.
They even get the innocent
    To somehow get involved.

I'm sure they have their followers
    In every single group.
The one who's causing problems is
    The leprechaun's own dupe.

They might seem very innocent
    And smile with lots of charm,
But they are filled with viciousness.
    Their mouths will cause much harm.

Beware of trouble makers then
    In any group or cause.
Don't let them ever take you in
    Or maul you with their jaws.

The Banshee

The Banshee, women fairy folk,
    A death can prophesy.
They wail and weep near Irish homes,
    For those about to die.

They visit only Gaelic homes,
    Descendent sons of Mil.
If your name starts with "O" or "Mac,"
    Put ear to windowsill.

And listen close that you might hear
    The Banshee wail and weep.
And if you hear their solemn dirge,
    A prayerful vigil keep.

But if the Banshee's silent,
    Breathe peacefully and cheer.
And knowing that you've got more time,
    Go out and have a beer.

The Banshee are a warning then
    That someone soon will die.
Let's hope that when we hear them wail,
    It is not you nor I.

The Celts Return to Europe

In the 6th century A.D. the Irish Celts again invaded Europe, not as warriors but as missionaries. They returned to the continent to restore the faith that Germanic tribes had all but wiped out. Although the Celtic culture had vanished from Europe with the conquests of Caesar centuries before, it had been preserved in all its purity and richness in Ireland. There Celts held on to their language, their art, their spirit and traditions. When Irish missionaries were sent back to Europe to teach and preserve the faith, they also brought back to Europe their many Celtic treasures.

The Celtic love of wandering was most conducive to missionary activity and brought them in great numbers back to Europe. The Celtic missionary church was often at odds with the Mother Church in Rome. The Celtic church was organized like the Celtic tribe, austere and highly individualist. The tribe was mirrored in monastic life more so than in the bishopric. The Celtic love of learning and poetry and their unique feelings for art and design found a patron in the monasteries, while Celtic distrust of authority somehow found a focal point in the local bishop. The many manuscripts and illuminations of this age were highly influenced by Celtic culture as the lives of saints were highly influenced by Celtic exaggeration.

The Mission Invasion

The Celtic love of wandering
    Made Irish mission-minded,
Far more so than in Italy,
    Where they were mission-blinded.

Celts came to Europe once again,
    After the fall of Rome.
As missionaries to the west
    To bring the faith back home.

Since Celtic culture of that age
    Colored the Celtic Church.
Society based on the tribe,
    Swept bishops off their perch.

Monastic life was family,
    Whose father was the abbot,
A pious version of the tribe
    That it influenced while at it.

The ultimate in sacrifice
    Was giving up the tribe.
The hermitage evolved from this,
    A cross God's love prescribed.

A bishop didn't seem to fit
    Into the Celtic plan.
So abbot and the Irish monks
    Made him an "also ran."

Fun with Irish Myths

All Celts loved works of bravery
    And great heroic deeds.
So lives of Saints were much revered,
    Fulfilling Celtic needs.

The Celt imagination was
    A bit exaggerated.
When focusing on lives of saints,
    Good sense was abrogated.

And even to this very day,
    The Celts are mission-minded.
In giving bearings to the West,
    That culturally got blinded.

While western art is stripped away,
    Replaced by white washed shell.
I'm sure the Celt is certain that
    All culture's gone to hell.

Or when great music of the past,
    Gives way to some guitar.
I'm sure the Irish sense of art
    Thinks things have gone too far.

Or when those pious practices
    That made their parents saints,
Are set aside as frivolous,
    It brings forth Celts' complaints.

Fun with Irish Myths

It is an age of silliness,
    When garbage is called food.
When trite is called aesthetic,
    The sensitive called rude.

The mini-minded are called bright,
    The dullard called the scholar.
Periti are those mindless men,
    Who parade behind their collar.

Barbarian iconoclasts
    Now pull the apple cart.
Felt banners of a mindless child
    Are somehow known as art.

In spite of all this nonsense, though,
    The Celts have kept their cool,
Just waiting to invade again,
    On mission to the fool.

Conclusion

There are so many Irish myths
    That we could still present,
But in the book before you,
    I think we've made a dent.

These Irish myths give clear insight
    Into the Irish mind.
You'll know the Irish better now,
    Unless you have been blind.

You've seen them at their very best.
    You've seen them at their worst.
You know what Irish blessings bring,
    Or what brings on their curse.

You've seen a loving people,
    That often times can hate,
A people that is stubborn, too,
    But can accommodate.

A people with a temper which
    They always must control.
A people that loves meat and spuds,
    But not in casserole.

A people bright and keen of wit,
    Renowned for memory,
Trained by their scholars of the past
    In every century.

Fun with Irish Myths

They love to drink, especially ale,
    And stay out very late.
Carousings mixed with boastfulness,
    Is sure an Irish trait.

There's nothing like an Irish joke,
    Told with the Irish wit.
They're very sentimental, too,
    Though this they won't admit.

And they are sure a humble lot,
    but don't want it to show.
They also are a bashful bunch,
    But don't want you to know.

But as you grow to know them well,
    You pierce their alibi,
Which sometimes makes them act quite rude
    To hide the fact they're shy.

I'm sure that you will know them best
    As very loyal friends.
They'll always be on hand to help.
    Their friendship never ends.